WE'RE
HAVING A
KITTEN!

WE'RE HAVING A KITTEN!

From the Big Decision Through the Crucial First Year

ERIC SWANSON

INTRODUCTION BY
ALLEN M. SCHOEN, D.V.M., M.S.

ILLUSTRATED BY BOB DOMBROWSKI

A HIGH TIDE PRESS BOOK

ST. MARTIN'S PRESS ❧ NEW YORK

For Lucy

Design by Doris Straus

Library of Congress Cataloging-in-Publication Data

Swanson, Eric.
  We're having a kitten : from the big decision through the crucial
first year / Eric Swanson ; illustrations by Bob Dombrowski.
    p. cm.
  ISBN 0-312-17062-9
  1. Kittens. 2. Cats. 3. Cat breeds. I. Title.
SF442.S9 1997   97-24682
636.8—dc21   CIP

First Edition: November 1997

10 9 8 7 6 5 4 3 2 1

TABLE OF CONTENTS

INTRODUCTION

The human/animal bond holds great fascination for me. As a holistic veterinarian, I have witnessed firsthand the profound spiritual bond that exists between people and their beloved pets. But I have also seen the disillusionment of that relationship when unrealistic expectations or half-hearted commitments were made. These animals often end up in the hands of shelters, abandoned, or euthanized.

We're Having a Kitten! is an excellent guide to the vital issues that should be considered *prior* to adopting a pet. The aim is not to discourage pet ownership, but to encourage a thoughtful decision, thereby increasing the chances of a happy union. Realistic expectations and a firm commitment are the first steps to a healthy marriage.

If you decide to take the plunge, *We're Having a Kitten!* will support you on your journey with valuable insights along the way. It will help you find a cat that's right for you, create an ideal environment that nurtures your new bond, and support you through the first crucial year. This is truly a holistic approach.

As a veterinarian, author, and animal lover, I am happy to recommend this book to all who consider sharing their life with a furry companion. Go forth, contemplate, and if it feels right, enjoy!

Allen M. Schoen, D.V.M., M.S.
Author, *Love, Miracles, and Animal Healing*

CHAPTER 1

Should We Have a Cat?

Chances are, if you're reading this, the question of whether or not to have a cat has crossed your mind more than once. This is quite natural. In the sphere of human activity, contemplation of a thing very often precedes doing it. A bit plodding and obtuse perhaps, but it's the way most jobs get done. If you decide to have a cat, you'll learn that the human way of doing things is not always the most efficient. Some people find this more difficult to accept than others, but cats are endlessly patient. Unlike other sorts of teachers, they never give up.

Perhaps you already have a cat, who is now perched on the back of the sofa watching you read this, wondering why on earth you're sitting so quietly when you could be doing something worthwhile, like licking your hindquarters or chasing a fly. You could try explaining that you need time to find out a few things before you're ready to launch into the serious business of playing, grooming, or napping. You could claim that it's like learning a new language — grammar and vocabulary come first, then conversation.

These attempts at being reasonable will fail, of course. Probably the best thing to do is to tear a piece from one of the blank pages in this book, crinkle it, and hurl across the room. Your cat will very likely leap from his or her perch and bat it around for a while, then settle in a nice patch of sunlight, content that you've mastered one of the first propositions of cat logic: Life without amusement is no life at all.

Of course, you might be thinking of getting this book for someone else who's considering a cat. In that case, you can probably skim through the text, which is not half as interesting as the pictures.

A BRIEF HISTORY OF CATS AND PEOPLE

If you find yourself wondering whether having a cat will truly enrich your life, you're not alone. People have been asking the same question for more than five thousand years. Obviously, each age and culture has phrased it somewhat differently. Ancient Egyptians probably asked something like, "O Great and Munificent Ra, you have taught us to store grains so that we will not perish in times of famine! Praise and Glory! We worship your great wisdom! Now, what are we to do about the mice and rats, who may also worship your wisdom, but are nevertheless devouring a goodly portion of our stored grain and soiling the rest with their droppings?"

Ra, known for his economical solutions, quickly dispatched *Felis libyca* — a small, brownish sort of wildcat — into the granaries of Egypt. The mice and rats may not have applauded this emanation of Ra's wisdom, but the Egyptians were certainly pleased. They held cats sacred, and built temples to a cat-headed goddess named Bastet. Harming a cat was punishable by death, as was any attempt to smuggle cats out of Egypt. It took all the skill of Phoenician traders to spirit cats across the border, and soon enough cats found their way into homes and granaries on all sides of the Mediterranean.

Over the next two thousand years, cats enjoyed a more or less honored place in civilized societies. Not every culture built them temples and special cemeteries, but most recognized their unique contributions to agriculture and housekeeping. As they adapted to more comfortable domestic environments, cats underwent certain physiological and psychological changes. They grew smaller and weaker, and developed distinct similarities to human infants — such as high, plaintive voices; round, limpid eyes; and warm, cuddly bodies. Whether this was a conscious ploy to manipulate human emotions will probably never be determined. Still, it is wise never to underestimate the intelligence of the feline species.

Unfortunately, this very intelligence became a dangerous commodity during the Middle Ages, when a kind of collective amnesia settled over Europe, and just about everything worth knowing was forgotten. During this period, we can perhaps see most clearly the distinction between feline and human evolution. Whereas feline development proceeds along extremely practical lines, human progress seems driven by laziness and envy: Whoever is wiser than his neighbor is weeded out. For hundreds of years, people hid their intelligence behind a false tolerance of bias and superstition. Cats, however, have traditionally refused to debase themselves this way.

In time, cats became associated with people who, because they could not or would not conceal their wisdom, were branded as witches or wizards. Merely to be seen speaking with a cat was enough to incriminate someone. Consequently, people living in the Middle Ages generally didn't ask, "Should we have a cat?" but rather, "Should we let our houses and barns be overrun by rats, or should we be burned alive at the stake?" Most people, understandably, found it more agreeable to lie down with rats.

They paid the price for convenience, though. As thousands of cats perished in the same cruel manner as their human familiars, the rodent population flourished; rats, in particular, carried the plague into hundreds of towns and cities. Naturally, the Black Death was possibly considered in some feline quarters as no less than a well-deserved comeuppance. The first outbreak wiped out nearly a third of Europe's population, and subsequent epidemics were no less devastating. Nearly two hundred years would pass before people realized that cats could take care of the problem, just as they'd effectively resolved the invasions of ancient Egypt's granaries. Though never quite rehabilitated to their former divine status, cats were once again welcomed into the human community.

Having learned from their misfortunes, modern cats are no longer as likely as they once were to flaunt their intelligence. Still, most of them remain mysterious, independent, and unpredictable creatures. Although in our more enlightened age people tend to find these qualities attractive, old superstitions persist. Very often the question "Should we have a cat?" masks deeper concerns about — for lack of a better phrase — the nature of the beast.

WHAT EXACTLY IS A CAT?
Cats defy intellectual analysis. This is probably why they've fascinated imaginative types for centuries. Egyptian artists celebrated the cat's divine origin in tomb paintings and sculpture. The Greeks stamped images of cats on their coins; the Romans depicted cats in mosaics and paintings, as well as on their pottery, coins, and shields. The most lavishly illustrated of all medieval gospels, Ireland's Book of Kells, contains several very nice portraits of cats and kittens in social situations; while Renaissance artists, such as Leonardo da Vinci and Albrecht Dürer, captured the lofty, spiritual aspect of the feline species for the edification of future generations.

Writers through the ages have also paid tribute to cats. Although the Old Testament doesn't mention them, the Babylonian Talmud describes their many useful qualities, such as cleanliness and hunting prowess. In *Alice's Adventures in Wonderland*, Lewis Carroll deftly caught the playful nature of feline wisdom in the character of the Cheshire Cat; Rudyard Kipling's short story *The Cat That Walked by Himself* examined feline self-reliance; and T. S. Eliot's *Old Possum's Book of Practical Cats* is a poetic salute to feline bravery, playfulness, gravity, and creativity.

It would be hard indeed to list all the fascinating qualities attributed to cats over the ages — especially since every cat seems to have a unique temperament. Nevertheless, most cats share a few common characteristics, which may be described as follows:

- Dignity
- Complexity
- Empathy
- Grace
- Presence
- Cleanliness
- Charm

A brief review of each characteristic will serve to deepen our understanding of these extraordinary creatures.

An Independent Dependent

Cats have received a lot of bad press about their supposed aloofness. Perhaps a more apt way to characterize this often-maligned trait is dignity. Cats have a very refined sense of boundaries. They may not always correspond to human expectations (standing on the dinner table, for example, is generally not considered uncouth in feline circles), but they are fairly well defined. Cats will not automatically assume that your life revolves around them. Just because you get up from the couch doesn't mean you want to play, or go for a walk, or give them a treat. They understand that people sometimes have other things on their minds.

They need to be fed, though, and longhairs especially need daily grooming. Cats also require a fair amount of mental stimulation. This doesn't necessarily mean you have to provide your cat with another cat to play with; a nice variety of toys will keep Lovey amused for a while. Even a paper bag or cardboard box can provide hours of enjoyment, as anyone who has ever made a fort out of an empty refrigerator box can attest.

Most importantly, even the shiest cat craves her owner's affection. While you're busy typing away at your latest manuscript or engrossed in a video, she may just crawl out from her hiding place under the bed and touch her nose to your bare foot, or rub her whiskers against your shin — just to make sure you're there. She might sit on your printer or your desk and watch you work. As far as she's concerned, you are Mommy, Daddy, God, Best Friend, and Sibling all rolled into one; and if she sometimes seems annoyed with you, just remember how long you spent in therapy trying to deal with your feelings about important figures in your life. Of course, if you prefer a more self-sufficient companion, you don't have to pick her up, or stroke her fur, or croon sweet nothings in her ear. She'll get the point. Just don't expect her to come running the next time you need a friend.

A Complex Companion

Cats have very sophisticated emotional lives and enormous willpower. When they want something, they're capable of devising all sorts of subtle or direct strategies to get your attention, which can range from simply staring at the back of your head until you turn around, to sitting on top of the book or newspaper you're reading. Sometimes all they want is some special sign of affection. For instance, Pumpkin's dish may be full, you may have scratched her behind the ears until your hand is ready to fall off, but she keeps right on giving you a round, insistent stare or meowing her fool head off. Finally, it hits you: She wants popcorn. She wants to watch *The Lady and the Tramp*. She wants you to run around the living room trailing a piece of string. After a few minutes of gratification, she'll probably walk away contented. You've done her bidding.

Jealousy and possessiveness are not uncommon, either. Cats are profoundly territorial. They mark both their living spaces and their loved ones with scent glands located in their paws and around their whiskers; nonneutered adult males, especially, will often mark their territories with urine, which is probably one of the best reasons to have them neutered in adolescence. Since their human companions have an annoying tendency to wash telltale scents with soap and water, or cover them up with colognes or air fresheners, a cat will spend a good part of his day reasserting his claim on furniture, walls, and people. While it may look like he's demonstrating affection, he's actually establishing ownership.

A cat will often attach himself to one person in particular, and ignore or merely tolerate other people in the house. Should you introduce a new person, an infant, or — heaven forfend — another cat into your home, he may react aggressively. This is usually caused by a fear of being displaced by the newcomer. A little extra cuddling and sweet-talking, and a generous portion of treats, will help mollify his feelings. Don't expect a cat to welcome a newcomer with open paws, though. He doesn't like to share.

At times, your cat may act like an spoiled brat, yowling around the house, or toppling the ceramic vase from your Aunt Gilda (which you never liked anyway) just because he's bored. At other times, he'll like nothing better than lying by your side on the couch for hours on end — until a fly swoops by, and then you might as well not exist. One loud noise can terrify him for hours, but he will fearlessly defend his territory against invasion by another pet, a visitor, or even you. And as he grows older, he'll exhibit many of the same characteristics as an aging person: insomnia, crankiness, an increased need for attention, and even a tendency to ramble just to hear himself talk.

Though adaptable to just about any situation, cats like routine. They like to be fed at the same time every day, to sleep in the same spot at night, and to hang out in a few select areas of the house or apartment. Change of any sort can produce stress, anxiety, and even surliness. They especially despise packing up and moving, which means going through the trouble of marking their new territory. Most cats make themselves scarce whenever the cat carrier comes out, since it usually signals some dreadful change in routine, which probably involves a lot of poking and prodding by the veterinarian.

Once your cat has accepted a change in her circumstances — whether it's a new home, a new sofa, or a new person in the house — her normal personality will usually reassert itself. Some cats are delicate or timid by nature, however, and any change is apt to be seen as betrayal. They'll want to forgive you, but they just can't get past their anxiety and resentment. Nervous cats need a great deal more tenderness to recover from the shock to their systems. This may tax your patience, but the result of pampering and coaxing is infinitely preferable to living with an angry ghost.

A Friend in Need

At times, cats seem like hairy little people. They may look at you with total understanding when you're confused. In times of sickness or sorrow, they may wrap your head in their paws, nuzzle your neck, or lick your cheek. They'll even act silly if the situation demands, chasing their own tails or rolling around on their backs. This doesn't necessarily mean cats are psychic or especially empathetic; they don't recite the St. Francis prayer before breakfast. They are, however, quite sensitive to changes in their environment, and a calm atmosphere is deeply linked with survival. If you are upset or ill, your cat will do whatever it takes to soothe you, so that his home becomes safe and secure once more.

Poetry in Motion

Grace, like dignity, is a defining feline trait. In fact, it's commonly believed in some circles that cats are actually aristocrats who were very naughty in their former lives. The feline walk is supremely regal: tail erect and whiskers forward. They can wrap their sinewy bodies around the most unlikely objects without tying themselves in knots or tipping over. They almost always land on their feet when they leap or fall, and even hefty cats can launch themselves from floor to counter with surprising alacrity. When stalking, they can make their bodies amazingly compact; yet they're never so intent on their prey that they can't occasionally stop and sniff the air, listen to a far-off sound, or pose for a spontaneous photograph.

Prolonged spells of clumsiness are usually a sign that all is not well, and the services of a veterinarian should be promptly sought. Incidental clumsiness, however, may simply reflect your

cat's attempt to amuse you or himself. And occasionally, even the most adept feline will forget himself when he hears the electric can opener, and tumble awkwardly off the couch in a mad dash for the kitchen. If he sees you watching, he'll likely stop, lick his paws, and give you a look that says, in effect, "I did that on purpose." When this happens, it's best to play along.

A Presence in the House

It's nice to come home sometimes and be greeted by someone who cares enough to say hello, but doesn't necessarily hang on your slightest word. A pat on the head, a lump of food, a casual question or two — that's enough for most cats. You both have things to do; the important thing is that you're both aware of each other's being. Still, some cats prefer a bit more attention, and will follow you around until you pick them up and cuddle for a few minutes. This type of behavior is usually encouraged by people who prefer a bit more attention themselves. Cats are also nice to have around at night, especially if you've been reading a murder mystery or watching a vampire movie on television. Cats are extremely sensitive to the sounds and scents that are beyond the normal range of human perception. The next time you find yourself shivering under your sheets, take a peek at your cat. If he's sleeping contentedly, there's not a vampire for a hundred miles.

The Easiest Toilet Training in the World

You don't have to paper the floor. You don't have to buy diapers or worry about cats telling their psychiatrists about your frustration and cruelty. You don't have to go for walks in rain, sleet, or dark of night. All you have to do is buy a plastic dishpan, a bag of litter, and a scoop. Show the cat where the litter box is, and maybe gently lift her inside. End of toilet training.

There are only two rules you should observe after introducing your cat to her litter box. First, don't place her food and water in the vicinity; unlike Hollywood agents, cats don't like to eat where they do their business. Second, scoop out solid waste at least once a day. Of course you'll forget sometimes, or go away for a long weekend. It happens. Just remember that cats don't like dirty toilets any more than you do, and aren't above demonstrating their displeasure in the most pointed manner.

Membership in the Society of Cat Owners

If you've ever envied people who pass around photos of their children, their new house, or their vacation in Jamaica, now's your chance to shine. Cats are extremely photogenic. They do a lot of funny, touching, and interesting things, which can almost always be described without offending or boring your listener. Cat stories make especially wonderful icebreakers at parties where you don't know anyone except the host or the person who dragged you there. And if you happen to start talking to someone who has cats (or has ever had cats, for that matter), you can count on a sympathetic ear. People who have cats are the luckiest people in the world.

WHAT ELSE SHOULD WE KNOW?

Reasonable people understand that whatever brings joy into their lives also brings commitment. Unfortunately, most people become entirely unreasonable around cats. They see only cuddly, soft creatures, and forget about the responsibilities involved in taking care of them. If you're thinking of having a cat, you ought to consider the following factors before making up your mind:

- Feline Longevity
- Your Personal Freedom
- Expenses
- Your Attachment to Possessions
- Temperamental Differences
- Nocturnal Habits

If you aren't prepared to meet a cat's physical and emotional needs, then you shouldn't have a cat. Animal shelters are full of abandoned cats. People use any number of excuses to get rid of them — some valid, many not. In most cases, they aren't fooling anyone. It's painfully obvious that they just got bored when their kitten grew up, or annoyed because their cat doesn't act the way they'd like him to, or tired of the commitment.

Of course, the arrival of a newborn, asthmatic children, or landlords who don't allow cats can pose serious dilemmas for cat owners. They are not, however, an excuse for dumping a cat in the woods or along the side of a road. While cats are great hunters, they don't know much about traffic; neither can they thrive in wet or freezing weather, or on a diet of garbage. In most cases, abandoned cats suffer cruelly and die very painfully. If you must give away your cat, try to find a loving home for it; if that fails, bring him to a reputable shelter.

If you should find an abandoned cat, the best course is probably to take him to the nearest shelter as soon as possible. Though his gratitude at being rescued may win your heart, it's usually not a good idea to take a cat into your home without at least some idea of what you're getting yourself into.

A Twenty-Year-Old Cat Is Not Unusual

According to legend, cats have nine lives. While a detailed analysis of reincarnation is beyond the scope of the present book, it should be noted that myths and legends often have some basis in fact. The nine-lives tale probably refers to cats' amazing agility, strength, and recuperative powers. They have been known, for example, to land on their feet after falling from very high places. (This doesn't mean you can leave your windows open without screens, however. Tips on safeguarding your home will be discussed in Chapter Four.) They can fight with other animals, perhaps losing an eye, an ear, or part of their tail, but otherwise walking away with their dignity intact. With proper treatment, they can even survive devastating illnesses or accidents.

An average cat can live anywhere from twelve to fifteen years — or longer, depending on his constitution. That's twelve to fifteen years or more of keeping cupboards stocked, choosing cat-friendly residences, and finding partners who share your enthusiasm. Still, you'll enjoy many of the same benefits available in any long-term relationship, not the least of which are a warm sense of familiarity and the gift of watching someone grow and change. You'll undoubtedly experience moments of frustration and ego-busting, as well. Cats have very strong opinions of how things should be done, and they won't always give in just because you're bigger and carry a couple of credit cards in your wallet.

It's Not Just Your Time Anymore

Having a cat doesn't mean your days of freedom are at an end. You can, for instance, decide on the spur of the moment to go away for a long weekend. Just be sure to leave a good supply of water and dry or semimoist food (canned food tends to dry out); and fill the litter box with fresh litter. Rocky may present his backside when you return, but his resentment will pass as soon as he hears the can opener.

Longer vacations require more forethought. You may decide to travel with your cat; appropriate arrangements will be discussed more fully in Chapter Five. If you choose to leave your cat home, you'll need to arrange for someone to come over and feed him, and clean out his litter box. You should also make some sort of arrangement with a friend or relative, in case an emergency keeps you away from home for a while.

Your daily schedule will undergo some adjustment as well. Maybe you're used to coming home after a long day and flopping on the couch, or reading your mail, or checking the phone machine. However, Spike will want food or attention — or both — before you're allowed to go about your routine. If you work at home, you'll probably find he gets bored with his toys and wants to play with you. And if you're an early riser, you can forget about sleeping late on occasion. Unless you keep Zimbra out of the room, she'll be pushing your eyelids open with a velvet paw at six A.M., or whenever you normally serve breakfast.

From time to time, too, cat emergencies will demand attention. They may range from the comparatively minor (running out of food) to the absolutely critical (illness or accidents). You might be able to avoid a breakfast run by serving up last night's leftovers, but serious situations will require immediate action. Cats never cry wolf. They don't fake illness to win attention, or pretend to be hit by a car just to get out of doing something they don't want to do. Listlessness, persistent vomiting or diarrhea, fever, coughing, difficulty urinating or defecating, and any other unusual behavior require prompt veterinary attention.

Expenses

Though you won't have to save for college or worry about buying new shoes every six months, you will have to determine whether you can realistically afford to care for a cat. Expenditures fall into three distinct categories:

Ordinary expenses include food and litter. In the wild, cats tend to devour all of their prey — including bones, fur or feathers, and whatever happens to be in the victim's stomach. This economical approach to mealtime provides them with protein, minerals, roughage, water-soluble vitamins, and an odd assortment of glandular secretions. Some people enjoy preparing their own cat food, blending a variety of meats with bone meal, brewer's yeast, and vegetables. Others prefer to buy prepared food. These are the only options available to ensure your cat receives all the nutrients he requires. A steady diet of table scraps is not acceptable.

You can also expect to go through about two pounds of litter each week for every cat in the household. Many people find clumping litter more convenient and less likely to retain embarrassing odors than the nonclumping variety. Avoid using litter that contains odor-controlling or odor-masking ingredients, though. Cats and people alike inhale litter dust, and chemical additives that control odor can prove toxic over time.

Common veterinary expenses include yearly checkups, immunizations, and neutering or spaying. While these will be discussed more thoroughly in Chapter Six, bear in mind that immunization and tests for common feline diseases are absolutely essential — not only for the cat, but for the people around her as well. Cats can carry viruses, fungi, and other unpleasant parasites that may be hazardous to human health.

Extraordinary veterinary expenses may be incurred if your cat is injured or develops a serious illness, such as cancer or Feline Urologic Syndrome (FUS). Depending on the treatment involved and the length of time your cat has to spend at the vet's, costs can rise quite dramatically. Fortunately, pet insurance is now available from several sources. Your veterinarian or your local animal shelter or animal hospital should be able to advise you about insurance carriers. A more complete discussion of insurance can be found in Appendix B.

How Much Do You Love Your Things?

When it comes to worldly possessions, cats seem to have mastered the Buddhist art of nonattachment. They will cheerfully vomit hair balls on your prize kilim, track litter across your faux-grained floor, and gnaw the blooms off your African violets. They don't care if they shed on cashmere or cardboard, and anything small or light enough to bat around for a while is fair game for amusement. None of this is calculated to infuriate you; it's just ordinary cat behavior. After all, some of the things people do without a second thought, like taking a bath or brushing their teeth, seem downright appalling from a feline perspective.

Probably the most distressing cat behavior involves clawing the furniture. It's also the hardest to control, since clawing serves both to sharpen the cat's primary means of defense and to mark his territory. Nevertheless, even this behavior can be redirected if you're willing to invest some time and effort. We'll explore training techniques in Chapter Six. Meanwhile, you should know that Princess may not immediately digest what you teach her, and that even after learning that the expensive post you bought her is an appropriate scratching tool and your new Louis Vuitton luggage is not, she may not be able to resist an occasional swipe when your back is turned.

Strange Fits of Passion

Feline moods are unpredictable. Your cat may be dozing peacefully in her favorite chair, and then suddenly decide it's time to rehearse her audition for Cirque du Soleil, running like mad across the hardwood floors and bouncing off the furniture. Or she may take umbrage one morning at your sudden burst of affection. After all, who likes being swung in the air by some big galoot who insists on planting coffee-scented kisses all over her face?

Cats are not uncritical. They may despise your favorite sweater, completely ignore the toy you spent half an hour choosing, and one day decide that the food you've been serving them for the past three years is irredeemably disgusting. Some cats may wander around the house meowing forlornly if you're away, and treat you like a leper when you return. Don't count on them to like all your friends and loved ones, either. Little Lucy may adore your friend Madge, and stalk your mother without mercy.

Frightening experiences can undermine your cat's confidence for days, months, or even years. Where once she enjoyed lounging regally in the sunlight, she may now spend the greater part of the day holding court with shadows under the bed. Prolonged or severe stress can lower her tolerance to disease, or precipitate some other medical problem.

Finally, because her feelings run deep, she may grieve the loss of a human or animal companion — which will be all the harder for her to bear because she won't understand why her friend has suddenly disappeared. If she pines or pads around the house meowing inconsolably, you'll need to give her lots of special treatment. Whatever time you spend comforting her will help you through your own grief as well.

Nocturnal H(a)unting

Cats are nocturnal prowlers. Though they can't see in complete darkness, they're better suited for nighttime hunting than many other animals. They also nap a lot during the day, which can make them awfully peppy just when your fancy turns to thoughts of sleep. You can try to curb Buster's tendency to romp around by putting away his toys before you go to bed. He has such a fantastic imagination, though, that just about anything is fair game for a midnight tackle. Your feet twitching under the covers make a particularly appealing target; so do shiny things, like jewelry or coins. Piles of paper, pens and pencils, and open garbage cans are also perennial nighttime favorites.

Since the point of hunting is to catch something lovely to eat, a bedtime snack can often help to quell your cat's nocturnal urges.

Likewise, a bracing game of tag or chase-the-mousie just before turning in will burn off excess energy. As a last resort, you can try putting your cat in a separate room at bedtime. Just make sure his litter box and water dish are in the same room, along with a few squishy toys that won't make a lot of noise when he bats them around. Even so, you may be awakened in the middle of the night by angry or distressed yowls. After all, playing alone isn't half as much fun as playing with you.

In time, your cat will adapt to your sleeping habits. The chance to curl up next to something warm, and let someone else worry about hunting, is usually too good to pass up. However, you may find that the place Bruce has chosen to settle is a bit awkward for you. If so, gently pick him up and move him to another spot on the bed; in the most loving possible way, let him know it's not a matter or rejection, but mutual comfort. He'll probably sneak right back as soon you're snoring, but at least you won't spend half the night fretting about your legs pinned under twelve pounds of blissfully sleeping cat.

WHERE DO WE FIT IN?

People are just as complex as cats; they're just less honest about it. Before you decide to have a cat, it's a good idea to take stock of your life. Try to see yourself in the worst possible light. A realistic inventory of your situation and personal habits is your best guide in deciding whether or not to have a cat.

Your Job

In many respects, cats make marvelous companions for busy people. They don't have to be walked or (with the exception of long-hairs) extensively groomed. There are no cages to clean or tanks to refill. Although they look forward to regular mealtimes, you can leave food and water for them, and they won't gobble it down all at once and pace around for the rest of the day worrying where their next meal will come from. Most will happily stay inside the four walls of a studio apartment for the rest of their lives, as long as someone's around at least part of the time.

If more than one person shares your household, your cat will probably receive the human affection and interaction she needs when you're not around. If you live alone, though, long, lonely days with no one to talk to can begin to wear on even the most self-centered feline. Like the medieval ladies whose warrior husbands left them alone for years in dreary castles, your cat may go quietly mad. If you work long hours, you'll have to compensate for the time you spend away from home by giving her lots of attention when you return — something you may not want to do if you walk through the door exhausted and irritable after a hard day at the office. You may even consider the possibility of having two cats, so they can keep each other company while you're out earning catnip money.

Travel

If your job requires a lot of travel, you should definitely make arrangements for someone to look in on your cat once or twice a day while you're out of town. Prolonged or repeated absences on your part will cause your cat a great deal of stress, though; just because Max can't threaten divorce or insist on couples therapy doesn't mean he won't express his deeply wounded feelings some other way. If you're away more than you're home, he'll become anxious, possibly destructive, and probably ill.

If you travel only occasionally, you may decide to take your cat with you. Cats who become accustomed to traveling at an early age adapt especially well to family vacations, but even older cats have been known to enjoy a change of scene once in a while. You'll need to make sure ahead of time that the place you're staying allows cats; since most hotels frown on four-footed guests, it's not really feasible to take your cat with you on a three-day business trip to Chicago. However, a trip to your Aunt Millie's country house might be a happy adventure, as long as Aunt Millie likes cats, and doesn't have any of her own that might resent another feline encroaching on their territory.

Should traveling together prove impossible, and if you can't arrange for someone to stay or visit your cat, you'll need to board her. The home of someone who likes cats, and perhaps is already acquainted with your cat, would be the ideal setting; otherwise, you'll have to board her at a cattery or the vet's. From a feline point of view, this is the least pleasant option. Imagine yourself in a three-foot-square cage, surrounded by a bunch of noisy, smelly strangers, and you'll understand why your cat may be resentful when you come home tan and rested from a week in Barbados. In Chapter Six, we'll look more closely at the issues involved in traveling with your cat and boarding her.

Children

Cats and children make excellent companions. Cats are small and extremely nice to hold. Children easily relate to a cat's playfulness and curiosity — probably because they share the same qualities, until horrid things like social studies and gym class knock the wind out of their sails. Helping with the cat's care and feeding, meanwhile, helps to foster the illusion that responsibility can be fun.

If your cat has been the only "child" in the house for any amount of time, you may notice signs of jealousy when you bring a newborn home. This is a natural enough reaction: Many a human child has suffered pangs of anxiety with the arrival of a new baby. A cat's fear of rejection may be even stronger, because he won't necessarily grasp the full significance of all your patient explanations about the blessed event. When baby arrives, he'll probably be curious to see what all the fuss is about. Don't shut him out of the adventure of raising a child. He may sniff or even lick the little one, and watch rapturously from the sidelines while baby is being washed, fed, and changed. Then again, he might be bored to tears. He may just wait until the child is old enough to be interesting.

Whatever your cat's response, be sure to give him some extra affection after you put baby down for a nap. It's a good way for both of you to relax, and it also keeps him out of the room where baby is sleeping. With all due respect to the wisdom of old wives, cats will not suck the life's breath out of a baby. Nevertheless, infants are entirely helpless for the first few months. They can't move around much if a cat decides to snuggle in the crib.

As children grow up, they must be taught to play gently with the cat. Cats do not enjoy having their eyes poked or their tails pulled; nor are they noted for their willingness to be dragged around by their paws. Such treatment may injure your cat, or at least make him afraid or angry enough to retaliate. You'll need to keep an eye on all social interactions until you're sure all parties understand they must treat each other with respect.

People Who Just Can't Be Around Cats

Some people have very strong reactions to cats. If you live with someone who has allergies or some other physical condition aggravated by animal fur, there's no realistic way to have a cat. Confining your cat to a single room or area of the home will not solve the problem. Allergic reactions are typically caused by chemicals in feline saliva, which are released when cats lick their fur. When the saliva dries, these chemicals become airborne and penetrate an entire living space.

The issue becomes a little more complex if the person who can't be around cats doesn't actually live with you. You'll have to weigh the advantages of having a cat against the disadvantages of entertaining outdoors in January. Similarly, if you're presently single, you may face the dilemma of falling in love with someone who starts to sneeze around your cat, or simply doesn't like cats. It may be harder than you think to choose between human love and feline companionship. Still, history is full of men and women who have forsaken their friends for far less substantial reasons. Most of them end up badly, but that's another story.

Unless you're happily ensconced with someone who shares your attraction to cats, or unless you've committed yourself to a life of celibacy or solitude, you'll probably have to deal with one or another of these scenarios someday. Before you decide to have a cat, you ought to contemplate your options or responses. The answers may surprise you.

IS IT REALLY A CAT WE WANT?

If you're reading this book, you probably have at least some idea of the commitment involved in caring for an animal. Yet even the most thoughtful and nurturing person may not be ready or willing to meet the special demands of feline companionship. Cats are headstrong, surprising creatures; although perfectly content to surrender to the comforts of domestic life, they still remember their wild origins. This is the heart of their mysterious appeal.

Unlike hamsters, parakeets, and fish, cats neither need nor enjoy close confinement. Whereas dogs are pack animals, and instinctively obey the lead dog (which in a domestic situation usually means you), cats will not tolerate any attempt to dominate them, no matter how well-intentioned. Neither do they particularly enjoy group activities. While most dogs consider it a treat to go for a walk with their masters, cats find such things deeply humiliating.

The feline model of community resembles a solar system. Territories may overlap, and weaker animals may sometimes revolve around stronger ones, but by and large cats prefer to maintain a respectful distance between themselves and other creatures. They can never be wholly owned, nor will they expect to wholly own the person who cares for them. Unlike almost every other creature on earth, cats understand the dangers of complete dependency.

A QUESTIONNAIRE

If you still have doubts about whether having a cat is right for you, you might find it helpful to look at the following questionnaire. This is not a test. It's simply a way to clarify your attitudes and expectations so that you can answer the bigger question: Should we have a cat?

1. How well do you cope with surprises? If the cat who acted so feisty and independent in the adoption center suddenly starts following you around the house, crying for attention, can you deal with his need for affection? If he practically did somersaults to win you over in the store, can you handle the changeling who craves his independence once you bring him home? How do you feel about mood swings?

2. Can you put someone else's needs before your own? If you come home from an extremely long day and there's no cat food in the house, will you go back down five flights of stairs and walk seven blocks to the nearest grocery store or deli?

3. Would stepping in a pool of cat vomit first thing in the morning ruin your day? If your cat is sick or angry, and leaves a ripely smelling pile behind the television, would you want to punish him?

4. Do you spend a lot of time away on business or vacation? Do you plan on taking a three-year meditation retreat in the near future? Could you be transferred to a foreign country that might not admit cats or require a long quarantine?

5. If you don't own your current residence, does the owner or landlord allow cats?

6. Does someone you live with suffer from allergies or other ailments? What about close friends or relatives?

7. Can you afford regular immunizations and veterinarian visits, along with food and litter? Is your budget flexible enough to allow for medical treatments in case of an accident or serious illness?

8. Are you willing to rearrange your home so that precious but attractive furnishings are out of harm's way? Can you deal with the occasional broken vase, or cat hair on your dark wool suit? What about finding claw marks on your favorite chair, or cat hair on the dinner table?

9. Finally, can you sustain a relationship for the next ten or twenty years? Do you think you might get bored when your cat is no longer small and cuddly? When she's old and cranky, and her joints are sore and her eyesight fails, will you still be able to give her the same affection that flowed so naturally when she was a kitten?

While these questions aren't definitive, a majority of negative responses suggests that a cat may not be the most satisfying companion for you at this point. The world is full of interesting creatures, however; maybe another type of pet will serve your needs better. And at some point in the future, you may just find a place in your heart that's absolutely the right size and shape for a cat.

CHAPTER 2

Yes, We Should Have a Cat!

Congratulations on making it to the second chapter. Clearly you have an adventurous spirit and a capacity to extend yourself beyond the cozy sphere of self-interest. This particular set of traits is less common than you might think. Many people love animals, but are either unwilling or unable to make room for them in their lives; others don't mind taking personal risks, but aren't all that keen on sharing. While the Egyptian goddess Bastet rains blessings down on everyone, she shows particular favor to people who have spirit and compassion in equal measure.

She does not think highly of rash decisions, however. Cats come in a variety of shapes, sizes, and temperaments. People tend to be remarkably consistent. They are quick to assume their own needs are self-evident, and thus beyond the range of intellectual examination. Before scooping up the first cat to cross your path, it's wise to spend some time thinking about the sort of companion you'd like.

Among the factors to consider are:

- Your own temperament and expectations
- The feline qualities you most admire
- Breed-specific characteristics
- Your prospective pet's history and health

WHAT KIND OF OWNER ARE YOU?

It's not unusual for people thinking about adopting a pet to suddenly acquire all the impressive personal qualities of an Eagle Scout. In their mind's eye, at least, their patience becomes limitless. They can't remember having headaches or bad days. Reliability has always been their creed. Their compassion would make St. Francis hang his head in shame.

This sort of wishful thinking tends to ignore one of the most unsettling, and at the same time, the most gratifying, aspect of pet ownership: the element of surprise. Cats may be like people in many ways, but they are not people. They obey their own nature, which human beings can neither fully predict nor understand. No matter what kind of owner you'd like to be, you'll have to deal with a certain amount of unprecedented behavior.

Of course, the type and amount of surprise you can accept will depend on your own temperament, habits, and circumstances. The first step in deciding what kind of cat to get is to take a good warts-and-all look at yourself. Your peace of mind may hinge on a tidy household, for example. On the other hand, you may find a casual approach to housekeeping more congenial. Some people prefer a serene environment, while others feel bereft without a sense of activity around them.

Your age and physical condition are also important factors. Long-haired cats require daily grooming, which may be difficult for people who suffer from arthritis in their hands. Young or particularly active cats have a hard time managing their curiosity; they can dart out the front door faster than you can say Miranda, or shimmy up the curtains without necessarily formulating a plan for getting back down. Kittens, especially, are apt to disappear into cubbyholes and other dark regions of your home you never dreamed existed. It takes a certain amount of agility — not to mention patience — to hunt them down.

You'll also want to consider your daily schedule. Certain types of cats, like certain types of people, need a lot of attention. They like to talk; they need to be stroked or otherwise actively engaged. Think of Rapunzel sitting alone in her tower, day after day. It was sheer luck that the first stranger who came along was a handsome prince; she'd probably have run off with the village idiot if he'd come by first. So if no one's going to be home most of the day, you may want to consider a cat who doesn't require as much personal contact.

WHAT ARE YOU LOOKING FOR IN A CAT?

Whoever said "In the night, all cats are gray" can't have been a very discriminating individual. Even in the dark, some cats are blue, some are orange, some have stripes, and some have spots. One type, the Sphynx, has no fur at all — which should make it rather easy to identify, even blindfolded in a lead-lined basement several hundred feet below ground.

Altogether, slightly more than a hundred different breeds have been identified by animal societies across the world. Appearance, temperament, and care vary with each breed, of course. A sturdy American shorthair will feel much more solid in your lap than a wriggly little Abyssinian. Siamese cats, meanwhile, are known for their intelligence and conversational skills. For sheer luxury, nothing can match the placid Persian, who will need daily grooming — unless you prefer wading through clouds of cat fur, or waking every morning to the gentle sound of Puffy hacking up a hair ball.

Once you've examined your own needs and habits, think about the qualities your ideal cat would possess. Then take a look at Chapter Three, which examines feline characteristics by breed. It's not a bad idea to compare notes with a veterinarian or someone who has experience with the type of cat that seems to best suit your needs. Later on in the chapter, we'll discuss other sources of information and advice. For the present, a few general distinctions bear mentioning.

Playful Kitten or Sober Adult?

Only seriously disturbed people don't think kittens are cute. They have winsome little faces framed by enormous ears; their fur is fluffy and soft; they are infinitely curious and boundlessly playful. Even when they play hard, their tiny teeth and claws aren't capable of inflicting much damage. While learning how to use their bodies, they perform all sorts of funny, undignified stunts.

Kittens require a huge amount of supervision, however. They seem particularly drawn to all manner of tights spots, like open refrigerators and dishwashers, or cupboards filled with toxic chemicals. They are completely immoral when it comes to play, too, happily shredding houseplants, antique first editions, and just about anything else of value. For the first year of their lives, you'll have to play mother — which means teaching them "no," picking them up when they cry, and feeding them nice, soft food every few hours or so.

Older cats may not be as cute and funny as kittens, but they're far less demanding. They don't need to be fed or handled as often, and good habits have usually been established. Their temperaments are pretty much set by the time they're a year old; you can often tell by interacting with them for a little while whether or not your personalities will mesh. Finally, you probably won't have to invest as many years in taking care of an older cat as you would a kitten.

Poet or Athlete?

Some cats, such as Persians, Russian blues, and American shorthairs, are more sedate than others. They like to observe, preferably in a sunny place, out of the way of household traffic. As long as you feed them regularly and scratch behind their ears a few times a day, they won't make severe demands on your time. Every now and then, they'll chase a nice piece of string or a rubber ball. They'll rouse themselves to action, however, if food hasn't appeared in their dishes within fifteen minutes of their regular mealtime. In most cases, their strategy is simple but effective. They will plant themselves in front of you and stare. And stare. And stare some more.

Other breeds, such as Balinese or Somali, have more lively dispositions. They like to run around, climb things, and bounce off your furniture. They do not enjoy sitting on the sidelines, preferring instead to participate in everything you do. Some cats, like the Burmese, will literally stand on their heads to get your attention. Though athletic cats can be a joy to own, and will rarely let you down in front of company the way children can, they do not make ideal pets for people who collect delicate glassware or who regularly enjoy the challenge of intricate jigsaw puzzles.

Mixed Grill or Showgirl?

Generally speaking, the temperament and habits of purebred cats are easier to predict than those of mixed stock. Pedigreed animals have been carefully bred over generations to produce distinct physical and emotional traits. Most breeders, too, will allow you to visit their homes in order to observe how the kittens are being raised. This is a boon for any prospective owner, since the way in which a kitten is handled during its first few weeks of life has a decided impact on its attitude toward people. A home visit will also give you a chance to evaluate one, or perhaps even both, feline parents. Since character traits are often passed down from cat to kitten, observation of at least one parent can give some indication of what little Topsy will be like when she grows up.

Good breeding is not a guarantee of sound temperament, of course. Even the noblest bloodlines have been known to produce a black sheep now and then. Moreover, purebreds are expensive, especially if the animal you've set your heart on is the child of prizewinners. You can expect additional outlays if you decide to show your cat; the cost of pampering and pageants can add up over time.

One obvious advantage in acquiring a cat of humbler origins is a lower initial cost. Typically, you can expect to adopt a mixed-breed cat for the cost of its initial vaccinations and worming. Many animal shelters even arrange with local veterinarians for a free initial visit or free neutering.

In addition, mixed-breed cats tend to be healthier and more emotionally stable than their noble cousins. The unusual habits of human royalty are ample proof of the hazards of refinement.

Still, just because your little darling comes from good peasant stock doesn't mean she won't turn out mad as a March hare. If you decide to adopt a mixed-breed kitten, try to visit its home environment so you can watch it interact with the other members of the household. If you're adopting from a shelter or a pet store, ask about the cat's parents and previous owners; whatever you learn may shed light on your cat's personality.

Boy or Girl?

Gender-specific differences do not usually develop until sexual maturity. Nevertheless, many people believe tomcats are slightly more friendly than females. "Friendly" is a crude interpretation, of course, which cannot touch the nuances of feline cognition. In fact, timid toms and convivial queens are not as uncommon as people like to think. Though arguments concerning nature and nurture abound, the complexities of feline development will never be laid bare. They are a mystery, which can only properly be approached with respect and reverence.

Feline sexual behavior will be explored more fully in Chapter Six. Still, it is useful to note that, as they reach sexual maturity, males begin to mark their territory by spraying urine. The odor is unpleasant to everyone except the offending party, and is all but indelible. For this reason alone, it's a good idea to neuter a male cat at an early age — usually between six and nine months. Once the habit of spraying is established, even drastic measures may fail to curb it completely.

Choosing a Healthy Cat

A sick cat or kitten is a pitiful sight. Even someone with a heart of stone may be moved to care for an ailing animal. If you can afford the time and expense of nursing a sick cat, and have the strength to endure what may very well turn out to be a sorrowful conclusion, your reward in heaven will be very great. The task is not for the faint of heart, however.

Most people are not saints, and understandably prefer the joy of caring for a healthy animal. Whatever type of cat you choose, look for the following signs of physical well-being:

- Alert, responsive behavior
- A shiny coat
- Clear, bright eyes
- A clean, cool nose
- Clean ears
- Pale pink gums and tongue
- White teeth
- A clean bottom

Likewise, the following symptoms may indicate illness, abuse, or neglect:

- Pronounced droopiness or lack of interest
- Growling, hissing, or clawing
- Sneezing or coughing
- Discharge from the eyes, nose, or ears
- Excessive scratching of the coat or ears
- Bald patches
- Lumps or rashes
- Yellow or missing teeth
- Caking or pasting under the tail

If even one kitten in a litter you're examining exhibits some of these symptoms, you're probably better off looking elsewhere for a pet. Cats aren't apples, of course; one sick cat won't necessarily infect the whole bunch. However, cats can transmit a variety of diseases amongst themselves, and if one animal exhibits signs of poor health, it could be only a matter of time before the others follow suit.

WHERE DO CATS COME FROM?

Biological considerations aside, most cats come from people. Some people raise them for love, money, or love of money; some look away for a minute and discover to their horror that their darling Blossom has become a tart. Some people manage shelters or rescue operations; others are forced by circumstances to part with their companions. Even strays are often victims of human thoughtlessness.

Sources vary according to the people or organizations offering adoption. However, the most common channels may be broken down as follows:

- Homes
- Breeders
- Shelters
- Pet stores
- Veterinarians

Stray cats, by definition, usually come into a person's life quite accidentally. Although they can't be said to come from any particular source, the neglected children of Bastet will be discussed at the end of this section.

Homes

Most intelligent cat owners have their pets spayed or neutered (an option discussed in Chapter Six). Some either put the operation off until too late, or object to it on dubious philosophical grounds. As long as there are absentminded or fainthearted owners, the feline population will continue to grow. Regrettably, so will the number of unwanted cats.

Friends, neighbors, and business colleagues may know of someone who has kittens or an adult cat in need of a good home. Pet supply stores, shelters, and veterinarian offices often post adoption notices, as may libraries, community centers, or other public areas. Newspapers may carry listings for "pet sales" or "pet adoptions."

Acquiring a cat directly from a home is an ideal situation. It allows you to interact with your prospective pet at some length, observe its interaction with other members of the household, and to evaluate its behavior around furniture, plants, and so on. If you're getting a kitten, take the time to play with the whole litter; that way, you can tell whose personality best matches your own. You'll probably want to avoid overtly aggressive or timid cats, unless of course one of these is what you have in mind.

Mixed-breed cats and kittens can usually be acquired free of charge, or else for the cost of any prior immunization, worming, or other treatments. Not all owners go to the trouble of immunizing kittens, however, so you'll want to inquire up front. Don't be bashful. In the case of an adult cat, ask for any paperwork pertaining to his or her vaccinations and medical history; if it's not available, get the name of the cat's veterinarian, from whom you can usually obtain copies of important records. If the owner has never taken the cat to a vet, undetected medical problems may manifest later on. You may want to consider looking elsewhere.

Breeders

As mentioned earlier, purebred cats are somewhat more expensive than ordinary cats. Costs vary according to breed, lineage, and the amount of profit the breeder wants to earn. Not all breeders are reputable, however. To find trustworthy breeders in your area, contact the American Cat Fanciers Association (CFA), listed on the next page, or any of the similar organizations listed in Appendix A. Attend cat shows in your area, too, and talk to owners. Read through a few issues of magazines such as *Cat Fancy* or *Cat Fancier's Almanac*. If your local library or bookstore doesn't carry them, contact information is listed in Appendix A.

If you're thinking of showing your new cat, make sure it meets the requirements set up by cat show organizations. For the latest specifications, contact the American Cat Fanciers Association at the following address:

The American Cat Fanciers Association
P.O. Box 203
Point Lookout, MO 65726
Tel: (417) 334-5430

Upcoming shows are announced in various magazines dedicated to cat fanciers. However, even if you don't intend to show your cat, you should definitely ask for its registration certificate (also referred to as a pedigree or papers), which will verify your cat's genealogical history. You'll need this certificate if you intend to breed your pet.

Shelters

Without question, a shelter or rescue organization is the most humane place from which to adopt a cat. These animals desperately need homes, and, unless extraordinarily abused, will usually reward you with daily doses of affection and gratitude. If you have accumulated a substantial karmic debt during the present or any prior lifetime, a goodly portion of it will be cleared by adopting a shelter cat.

Shelter cats come from a variety of different backgrounds. Some have been rescued from a life of hell on the streets; some belonged to people who changed their minds about having a cat; some have been separated from their owners by the cruel hand of fate. The facts of a cat's prior history will likely be scanty, but most shelter workers will happily pass on whatever they know. Since animals are routinely examined, immunized, and wormed upon admission to a pound or shelter, you can at least count on adopting a healthy cat. Very young kittens may not have been immunized, however, since most vaccinations can't be given before the baby is eight weeks old.

The cost of adoption is often minimal, usually covering the paperwork involved. Consider it a donation to a worthy cause, and another star in your heavenly crown. Most shelters are listed in the telephone book. However, if you can't find a local listing, you may wish to contact the Humane Society of the United States or the American Society for the Prevention of Cruelty to Animals (ASPCA), as listed below:

The Humane Society of the United States
2100 L Street NW
Washington, DC 20037
Tel: (202) 452-1100

ASPCA
424 East 92nd Street
New York, NY 10128
Tel: (212) 876-7700

Pet Stores

You pass a pet store window and see a group of kittens frisking about, or perhaps one lonely youngster gazing longingly through the glass. Your heart melts. Parental instincts stir. Forces you don't understand whisk you inside the store, where you collar the first salesperson you see.

Before making any rash decisions, take a deep breath and look around the store. Is it clean? Does the cat in the window have a lot of toys to play with? Does the litter box seem fresh or appalling? More often than not, a filthy or disorganized pet store signals a proprietor who doesn't really care about animals. You're better off shopping somewhere else. You might even consider contacting the ASPCA to report unsavory conditions.

If the store looks clean enough, and the cats seem lively and well-attended, talk to the salespeople. If they can give you advice on selecting an appropriate animal, chances are even better that you're dealing with a reputable place. Ask about the cat's diet and medical history; find out as much as you can about where it came from. When buying a purebred cat, make sure it comes with papers. If papers aren't available, it's probably not a purebred cat.

This is not a tragedy in itself, but it does rather cast doubt on the store's respectability.

Veterinarians

Many veterinarians allow pet owners to post adoption notices in their offices. This does not mean, however, that the vet endorses a particular owner or can vouch for the health and well-being of the cats or kittens being offered. But it doesn't hurt to ask the receptionist, very nicely, if the animal in question happens to be one of doctor's patients. Some veterinarians do occasionally offer stray or abandoned animals for adoption. In this case, you can pretty much expect the cat or kitten to be healthy. As an added bonus, little Ralph or Lizzie will have already developed a nice relationship with the vet, so you won't have to bribe them with catnip every time their yearly physical rolls around.

A Few Words About Strays

You might wake up one morning to a find a tom camped out on your front porch, or a queen delivering kittens in your garage. You could be hurrying home on a rainy night and encounter a pair of glowing eyes. Forewarned is forearmed, however. Cats born in the wilds of city, town, or country often have a feral streak, and won't take kindly to being approached or handled. Some initial wariness is to be expected of any stray, but if a cat growls or hisses when you approach, you're better off calling the ASPCA or a rescue organization. More important, because a stray may not have been immunized against rabies, you absolutely must protect yourself against clawing, scratching, and especially biting. The rabies virus is usually passed though the saliva of an infected animal. If you're bitten by a cat you don't know, see a doctor immediately. Rabies is fatal: Only prompt medical attention can offer any hope of survival.

If Mr. Whiskers responds warmly to you, you should decide right away whether or not to adopt him. Remember that you

know nothing about him, and he may turn out to be a cad. If you don't feel comfortable committing for better or for worse, no one will blame you. Take him to a shelter as soon as possible, though, before he becomes attached to you. If you decide to keep him, immediately make an appointment with a vet for a complete physical examination and a series of vaccinations.

WHERE CAN WE FIND OUT MORE?

As with love, marriage, and plumbing, you can never really know enough about cats. Especially if you're considering a specific breed, you may wish to address a particular concern or decide between one or another type of cat. While you probably can't cover every single contingency, inspiration is available from a number of different sources.

Other Owners are probably the best source of advice and information on day-to-day living with a cat. Everyone's experience is a little different, of course, and you may hear contradictory tidbits here and there. Nevertheless, talking things over with several different owners should give you a pretty balanced picture of bringing up baby, whether baby is an ordinary housecat or a pedigreed beauty.

Books and Magazines offer detailed information on just about every aspect of cat care — from toilet training to holistic healing. Depending on the size of your library or favorite bookstore, the titles available may fill an entire wall or only part of a shelf. Naturally, while books can cover certain topics such as breeding or health care in great depth, magazines offer the advantage of timely information on topics as diverse as medical breakthroughs and cat shows.

CD-ROMs and Videotapes often manage to be instructive and entertaining at the same time. What they sometimes lack in specificity cannot compare to what they offer in terms of live-action footage of the proper method of introducing your cat to the toenail clippers or the extremely loathsome medicine capsule.

The Internet has recently evolved into an innovative format for delivering information on a variety of feline issues. If you have a computer, a modem, and an Internet service provider, you can browse the World Wide Web for cat-specific pages. Web pages sometimes change their address or disappear from the Web altogether; however, you may find some luck with OFF: Online

Feline Fanciers, located at: http://cesium.clock.org/~ambar/off/ or The Electronic Zoo at: http://netvet.wustl.edu/cats.htm. Online services such as CompuServe and America Online also sponsor forums for pet owners. Posting questions and reading messages in Usenet newsgroups, meanwhile, offer other means of learning more about cats. Like Web pages, newsgroups come and go, but rec.pets.cats. seems to have enjoyed a certain longevity.

Cat Shows can be a real hoot. Not only do they give you a chance to see cats in action — prancing, performing tricks, and occasionally misbehaving — but also serve to point out the enormous variety among cats of a particular breed. Owners, meanwhile, are usually open about the responsibilities and advantages of raising a particular type of cat.

Cat Clubs are responsible for organizing shows and for disseminating information on a particular breed or breeds. Most clubs are overseen by a cat registry, of which the three largest in the United States are the Cat Fanciers' Association, the International Cat Association, and the American Cat Fanciers Association. If you can't find a listing for a cat club in your telephone book, your veterinarian or local animal shelter may be able to direct you to those in your area. Otherwise, you can contact one of the registries listed in Appendix A.

THE ROLE OF INSTINCT
While choosing a cat requires forethought, undue agony should be avoided. There are no perfect cats. From time to time, Mittens or Nikita is bound to do something to irritate or disappoint you. These lapses from perfection are commonly known as Life, which cannot be ignored indefinitely. Actually, from an enlightened perspective, all cats are perfect, because they are exactly as they are.

Similarly, no amount of research can substitute for direct experience. You can read a hundred books and talk to scores of people, but don't discount the power of inexplicable attraction. Just as you're about to choose your new best friend from an adorable litter of puffy, lilac-point Himalayans, into the room might stroll a scrawny, cross-eyed alley cat with only half a right ear and a broken tail. Proudly wagging his crooked stump, he butts his head against your legs. His purr sounds as pleasant as a trash compactor, but there's something oddly comforting about it. You smile. He smiles. And now you're caught between all your careful deliberation and a powerful emotional yearning.

You may not face such an extreme scenario, but it's good to remember that your final choice may not rest solely on reason. If your head pulls you one way and your heart another, what are you to do? In such a case, the best thing is probably to close your eyes, take a deep breath, and silently ask the omniscient Bastet for guidance.

CHAPTER 3

Variations on a Cat

Not all relationships are perfect. Where members of the same species are concerned, any tragic mismatching of chemistries can usually be undone fairly simply through legal or other channels. At the end of the day, both parties can go home with their dignity reasonably intact. Sadly, the same cannot be said for interspecies associations. The acquisition of a pet is a lifetime commitment. There are no feline divorce courts.

Perhaps for this reason, people need to impose distinctions upon animals that would undoubtedly create a political stir if attempted on their fellow humans. Among animals, of course, the process of discrimination is usually handled without recourse to value judgments. Very simply, certain smells are attractive and certain others are not. People, however, must rely on a complex system of abstractions — which is simply a nice way of saying they resort to name-calling.

Different names trigger different emotional responses. Some of these responses may feel quite pleasant (beef Wellington, Mom's meatloaf, chocolate cheesecake); others may not (ammonia, IRS audit, Monday morning). Variations in response depend largely on upbringing, which is far too complex a subject to discuss at present. Suffice it to say that of the words most frequently used to describe cats, some appeal to particular individuals and some to others.

Curiosity

Most people have heard the saying "Curiosity killed the cat." Although this wise old saw has probably been applied more frequently to children than to other sorts of animals, it nevertheless serves to demonstrate that curiosity is the most widely recognized of feline characteristics. So pervasive is this thirst for knowledge that one might even call it a genetic trait. "Curiosity," however, misrepresents the true nature of the behavior it is meant to describe. It has more to do with hunger than with whether or not your earrings would look better on the floor than in the jewelry box.

Cats are carnivores; in the wild, particularly, they prefer freshly killed meat. And since no zebra worth its stripes is simply going to lie down and wait for the dinner bell, cats have to work hard for every meal. Hunting live prey requires constant alertness to the slightest sound or scent, and hours of watchful waiting for a nice young gazelle to wander away from the herd.

Yet while refined senses and boundless patience may be a cat's natural endowment, learning to use these gifts is another matter. Once they are sturdy enough on their legs, most kittens "practice" hunting each other. They learn to pounce, to bite, to wrap their paws around each other's heads and middles. Typically, once her kittens are strong enough to deal with live prey, a mother cat will bring a still quivering morsel home and show them, by example, how to kill. Later on, she'll bring live animals home and wait for her babies to give the coup de grâce. Anyone who has witnessed such a scene will undoubtedly notice the strong resemblance to classical Greek tragedy.

Once the kittens have learned how to kill, they're on their own. After staking out a territory where the eats are good, they'll defend it against other cats. This requires a daily patrol of the "fences" they've erected through spraying, rubbing, and occasional deposits of solid intestinal waste (politely referred to as "scats"). Even while resting, they'll usually keep a whisker out for any sign of poachers.

Naturally, a few thousand years of domestication is not going to undo a million years of evolution. Though the average house cat doesn't have to bring down a water buffalo or fight off a hungry lynx, his instincts are in no way blunted. He remains, rather, in a state of suspended development: possessing extremely refined senses, extraordinary alertness, and a biological urge to pounce, prod, rend, and bite, without necessarily knowing what to do with all these riches. After all, you provide a steady supply of food; and unless you've developed some rather peculiar tendencies, you're not likely to carry a terrified mouse in your jaws and show him the most effective way to snap its neck.

Thus, what people quaintly refer to as "curiosity" in cats may be better understood as the spontaneous activity of a finely calibrated hunting and killing machine. While perhaps not the most appealing point of view, it may help explain the often fascinating, sometimes annoying, and ultimately insuppressible behavior of cats. They won't knock your dentures off the bathroom counter because they want to play; they're looking for signs of life. They don't pace around the house because they're restless; they're just making sure that their territory is uncontaminated. Nor will they hop into an open cupboard just to be cute or exasperating; they're simply examining whether or not it is a likely source of food.

Not all cats express their curiosity with equal fervor. Kittens, as a rule, tend to explore their environment much more avidly than older cats. After all, without a mother to show them, they must learn through trial and error that loose change on the bureau is not especially tasty. On the other hand, knocking said change off the bureau may become an extremely effective means of encouraging slug-a-bed owners to present something a tad more palatable for breakfast. One must be very careful not to reward such innocent-seeming acts of coercion.

If you are looking for a particularly bright, inquisitive pet, you might want to consider adopting an animal from one of the breeds described below. Since cats seem to delight in proving people wrong in just about everything, this list should not be considered the final word; nor, indeed, should any of the lists in the sections that follow. There are well over ninety accepted breeds of cat, and a portrait of each would likely make the voyage at hand rather heavy going for anyone who does not consider *Ulysses* a light read. A more complete summary of feline clans can be found at the end of this chapter.

That said, the following breeds have been known to exhibit a marked inclination to leave no stone unturned in their quest for knowledge.

Balinese. The first of these engaging little snoops was born to a pair of registered Siamese. Like their parents, they had trim, athletic bodies, blue eyes worthy of a song, and pale fur highlighted with dark colors along the tail, ears, mask, and feet (commonly referred to as points). Whereas Siamese are known for their short coats, however, these kittens were draped in long, silky fur. Their graceful, undulating movements inspired some clever individual to name them Balinese, after the equally entrancing Balinese dancers.

At first, Balinese were considered genetic mutations, but as more and more long-haired kittens appeared, the CFA and other associations have accepted them as a distinctive championship breed. Their points are traditional Siamese colors: seal, chocolate, blue, and lilac. Since they require a good deal of amusement, it's a good idea to provide them with lots of toys. Otherwise, they are likely to select their own from among your prized possessions.

Javanese. Like the Balinese, Javanese cats are long-haired relatives of the Siamese. Their point colors are more exotic, however, ranging from pure deep orange to dappled brown and cream, to thick stripes of brown, red, gray, or blue.

Siamese. Though they could be described by any number of qualities, one feature that distinguishes Siamese cats from just about every other breed is their insatiable need to know everything. Do not for a moment think you can hide anything from these cats. They are keen thinkers, and will learn how to open doors and windows to find out what's going on. If you try to keep something from them, they will let you know exactly how they feel about your pathetic attempt at deception: Siamese cats are talkers, and their voices can rise to quite piercing levels when they're upset.

So persistently nosy are Siamese cats, and so quick to raise an alarm, that they were once employed as guardians of ancient temples. In modern times, with no divinities to protect, Siamese tend to elevate one member of the household over the others as a recipient of special attention. This can be a blessing or a pain, depending on how you feel about your privacy. Once they've made their choice, though, they almost never retract. Their hearts are far bigger than their bodies.

Singapura. Slightly less nosy than your average Siamese, Singapuras hail, not surprisingly, from Singapore. They began emigrating to the United States in the early 1970s. Typically, they are small creatures with wide hazel, green, or yellow eyes. Their coat is ticked, like a squirrel's or a gopher's; each individual hair shaft is made up of bands of different colors. Like little pitchers, they have big ears.

Singapuras are extremely affectionate, and bond very closely with their owners. They enjoy following you around the house, and sitting with you while you're watching TV or reading a book. However, they infinitely prefer sitting on your book, or between you and your TV — because you are nearly always the most fascinating item on their agenda. Having a Singapura is a bit like having a little brother or sister who looks up to you and wants to do everything you do. They're not codependent, however; when they know they're not wanted, they'll snoop around the house, collecting dirt they may or may not use against you at some future date.

Intelligence

All cats are blessed with some form of intelligence. Notice, for example, the clever way they've convinced people to take care of them. They don't have to go shopping, they don't pay taxes, and they never have to accept an invitation to a birthday party when they'd rather stay at home. They've even managed to hit upon a sublimely simple way of dealing with complicated remote control devices: Just swat them behind the TV stand and never think about them again.

Like Tolstoy's unhappy families, though, not all smart cats are alike. Some are very subtle, pretending to be silly or helpless in order to get you to do things for them. Some, amused by life, are content simply to watch the parade from a lofty perch, joining in now and again when the mood strikes them. Others delight in showing you how smart they are. If you have a yen to raise a prodigy without the expense of sending her to college, you might want to consider one of the following breeds.

Foreign White. Basically, these short-haired sweethearts are pure white Siamese. They have no point color at all on their tails, faces, paws, or ears. Most white, blue-eyed cats are deaf; not so the Foreign White. They have very keen hearing, which some people consider the basis of their extraordinary intelligence. Nothing escapes their attention.

Like the Siamese, Foreign Whites are lithe, athletic creatures, with very smooth coats. Their voices are not quite as piercing, though, and they tend not to react defensively over your occasional need for privacy. If you want to keep things from them, fine — they don't mind a bit of independence themselves. But they'll probably want to talk about what you were doing so long in the bathroom.

Malayan. Burmese in origin, Malayans are tough, medium-sized cats with thick, short coats. They are bossy geniuses who enjoy playing games more than just about anything in the world. Living with a Malayan is like living with Mozart; if you can handle his somewhat superior air, you will never lack for whimsy. The standard colors are tawny brown (champagne), blue, or silvery-gray (platinum). The blue variety tends to be a bit less smart-alecky than the platinum or champagne. Think Bach rather than Mozart.

Tonkinese. You may be tempted to think that a few stray human genes somehow found their way into the Tonkinese bloodline. These charmers have more character than they know what to do with, which can make them ideal companions for a single-person home. They enjoy intimate, one-on-one conversations and will happily take it upon themselves to supervise everything you do — offering comments and advice along the way. They have very acute powers of observation and recall, so if you're not sure whether you used three cloves of garlic or four in your last batch of stew, chances are your Tonkinese will remember.

Tonkinese are a hybrid of Siamese and Burmese cats. Their fur is soft and minklike, while their points tend to be darker variations of the rest of their coats. Though of medium build, they can feel quite heavy for their size. They also tend to be rather strong-willed and mischievous, so it would not be wise to keep a caged bird or a bowl of goldfish in the same house with them. You're apt to come home someday and find your beloved Tweety reduced to a couple of feathers stuck to kitty's mouth.

Like most highly intelligent creatures, Tonkinese need a great deal of stimulation. A lot of nice toys and an interesting cat tree (a climbing post with a series of shelves attached) can help keep them out of trouble while you're away or otherwise engaged. Ultimately, you may find that two Tonkinese will keep each other from getting bored and naughty.

Playfulness

As they mature, most cats settle down to very sober, responsible lives. A few exceptional breeds, however, never seem to lose their childish sense of fun. Just as certain types of high-spirited people can be uplifting and exasperating in equal measure, so these irrepressible felines may delight or vex their owners. They are endlessly inventive and a bit scatterbrained, and when one jumps out of your lap to chase something momentarily more appealing, you're not apt to take it personally.

Abyssinian. Though small, Abyssinians are practically fearless. They look like miniature mountain lions, padding swiftly from room to room; and like their wild cousins, they enjoy perching atop unimaginably high places. If they could only learn to dust, life with an Abyssinian would be perfect. Typical Abyssinians are slender, with a ruddy, ticked coat. They have enormous ears and almond-shaped eyes.

Less demanding than a Siamese, an Abyssinian nevertheless adores participating in all family activities. Board games can be particular favorites, since the little pieces are so amusing to bat around; but Abyssinians will happily learn any other game you care to teach them, especially if it involves fetching and retrieving. Because they like activity, they prefer larger accommodations to smaller ones. However, many Abyssinians have been known to enjoy taking an outdoor walk with their owners, submitting to a leash and harness in exchange for the chance to exercise and explore. Never use a collar; your cat could either slip out of it or damage his neck.

Burmese. "Laugh, and the world laughs with you" may well be the motto of this breed. While most other cats loathe teasing, Burmese don't mind being the butt of a good joke. In the nicest sense of the phrase, they are party animals who enjoy doing tricks — which can range from headstands to somersaults. They have even developed a characteristic sort of dance on their hind legs, often referred to as the "Burmese shuffle."

Burmese are round, compact animals, with small ears and full-moon eyes. Their fur is short and glossy, exquisite to the touch. Typically, their coat is deep brown, but selective breeding has produced some lovely blue- and cream-colored animals. One word of warning for anyone considering adopting one of these brilliant showoffs: They live for the rewards and praise they receive in return for their clever antics.

Korat. Though less maniacally precocious than either of the breeds mentioned above, the Korat (pronounce koh-*raht*) is an active cat with a lively disposition. Korats respond quite well to training, and enjoy playing games such as fetch the necklace and pounce the doily. They can even be trained to walk on a leash. Korats are typically silver-blue, with muscular, tense bodies. Their wee faces are nearly heart-shaped, which can tend to make their big eyes appear a tad hyperthyroid. Eye color can range from pure green to a greenish sort of amber.

Korats are fiercely loyal and have been known to demonstrate a certain degree of possessiveness toward the person (or animal) with whom they've bonded most closely. Loyalty is not without its price, though. Korats are not above demanding special attention from their chosen one, and they despise being left alone for more than a few hours. Still, because they are quite protective of their owners, you can usually rely on them to alert you to the arrival of visitors — especially those of the uninvited variety. With a Korat in your house, Cousin Edsel will never surprise you again.

Friendliness

Of course, not everybody wants a watchcat. Some people prefer their pets to demonstrate a few social skills. A cat who runs quivering under the bed every time the doorbell rings can be something of an embarrassment. Equally inconvenient is the cat who terrorizes your party guests. Strictly speaking, he may not intend to unsettle the boss's wife; as far as he's concerned, presenting one's buttocks for sniffing is a perfectly acceptable method of getting acquainted. On the other hand, he may actively resent loud voices, clumsy feet, and malodorous perfumes, and express his displeasure by way of a few well-aimed swipes with unsheathed claws.

If you're in the market for a pet that would pass muster with Emily Post, you might give some thought to one of the following breeds.

Bombay. The first Bombays were a hybrid of Burmese and black American shorthair cats. Like the Burmese, they tend to be round-bodied with small ears and large, wide-set eyes. Their soft coats are a deep, shiny sable color, and they tend to be heftier than their Burmese cousins.

Mixed heritage has somewhat tempered the Burmese tendency toward showing off. Bombays are gregarious, but not intrusive. Though they are perfectly willing to do tricks for company, you will not have to warn them more than once that your guests do not want to hear them play the theme from *Love Story* on the piano. Calm by nature, they adapt well to apartment living, yet they do prefer being the dominant cat in a household with more than one feline. Curiously enough, they will often accept a dog in the house more readily than another cat.

Ragdoll. As the name suggests, Ragdolls are wonderfully docile, floppy cats. They tend to be on the husky side, with broad chests and hindquarters. The average female weighs between ten and fifteen pounds; males range from twelve to twenty pounds. Though not precisely longhairs, they have coats that are quite full, and soft as rabbit fur. The fur around their neck and on the back of the hindquarters is usually longer than the rest, while their bushy tails rival Cyrano's panache. While their fur doesn't usually mat, they do require occasional grooming.

Ragdolls are pointed cats. The most common varieties are seal point, chocolate, lilac, and blue, although other varieties are becoming popular. As with other pointed breeds, their eyes are sapphire blue.

Ragdolls seem to have perfected the Buddhist ideal of non-aggression. If attacked, they will not defend themselves; when held, they relax completely. If you're looking for a cat you can count on to behave perfectly in any social situation, look no further. While Ragdolls love to be around people, and enjoy greeting guests at the door, they are extremely sensitive to individual temperaments. When they meet someone who fears or dislikes cats, they'll simply wish that person well and move on.

Birman. Few cats have as romantic a history as the sacred cat of Burma. According to legend, one hundred pure white cats lived in the Burmese temple of Lao-Tsun. One night, the temple was raided and the oldest priest was killed. At the moment of the priest's death, his cat jumped on his body and faced the golden, blue-eyed statue of the temple goddess. The priest's soul entered the cat, and as it did, the cat's white hair took on a golden cast and its eyes turned sapphire blue. Its legs, face, ears, and tail became earth-colored, as a reminder of death, while its paws remained white as a symbol of purity. A few days later, the cat died and carried the old priest's soul up to heaven.

As you may gather from the above tale, Birmans are light golden cats, with dark faces, ears, tail, and legs, and white "glove" paws. Their eyes are a deep, luminous blue. Their bodies tend to be large and stocky, covered with long, silky hair that doesn't mat, but still requires some grooming. The points are similar to those of a Siamese.

Temple life seems to have blessed the Birman with a gentle, easygoing personality and a hospitable attitude toward visitors. A Birman can be active and playful, but also knows how to be quiet during those periods when you happen to be meditating. They are basically sociable creatures, though, and can wax nostalgic if left on their lonesome too long.

Placidity

Although the modern age has witnessed a rapid disintegration of class distinctions, certain standards of behavior will probably remain firmly in place for a while to come. There is still a good deal to be said for qualities such as tact, dignity, and grace under pressure. Like well-mannered children, cats who know how to behave properly can offer their companions a deep sense of relief and satisfaction. Particularly for those who place high value on their personal or household effects, and for those who may be physically or temperamentally unable to devote a great deal of time to an active or emotionally demanding animal, a docile, sweet-tempered cat can make an ideal pet.

Placid cats are not incurious or unaffectionate; nor are they incapable of spontaneity. They simply tend to be more subtle in the way they go about things. Instead of chasing after the first dust bunny to blow by, they'll watch — and wait. Should a sudden need for reassurance overtake them, they won't necessarily leap on your lap or run through the house crying till you figure out what's wrong. They'll probably just glance winsomely in your direction, hoping to catch your eye. For these types of cats, spiritual communion is the highest form of creature comfort.

Persian. It's not hard to understand why Persians are the most popular breed of pedigreed cats in the world. For sheer opulence, no other cat comes close. Their long, flowing coats feel curiously alive to the touch; their wide, round faces express an innocence and sweetness unmatched by the more angular miens of their less regal brethren; their eyes, deep and richly colored, sparkle like the jewels of their mysterious, ancient homeland.

Persians have short, thick legs to support their broad bodies. Preferring the feel of solid ground beneath them, they generally refrain from jumping and climbing over delicate furnishings; similarly, they would rather eat rocks than climb your window treatments, no matter how inviting. Their favorite occupation seems to be posing, and they will happily drape themselves across a windowsill or chair for hours at a time, on the off chance that you may want to photograph or paint them. Of course, they have their impish moments. Persians are profoundly responsive to affection, and when lifted will often wrap their paws around their owners' necks, emitting grandiloquent, satisfying purrs. Some will even perform a sweet trick of sitting up on their hind legs to beg, looking for all the world like tiny bears.

Well known for their gentle dispositions, Persians adapt most readily to secure, contained environments. They make wonderful pets for apartment owners. However, they don't take kindly to teasing or rough handling, so families with young children may wish to consider placing little ones in a boarding school or detention center until they're properly trained.

Persians come in more than thirty different colors and patterns — including white, black, blue, smoke, tabby, calico, and tortoiseshell — suitable for just about any decorating scheme. They must be groomed daily. If left for any length of time, their fur easily becomes tangled and matted, a situation neither cat nor owner will find amusing.

Russian blue. As you might guess, these cats originated in Russia and their coats are a glossy, silky blue with silver tipping. Their remarkable color, complemented by emerald green eyes, has made them a highly prized breed indeed. Aristocratic in every sense of the word, they are long and slender in build, and their movements supremely elegant.

Russian blues are highly intelligent, quiet, and extremely sensitive creatures. Fastidious by nature, they only shed when they absolutely must. They don't mind playing with small (preferably expensive) toys, but unlike some cats, they are rarely, if ever, destructive. They bond tightly with their owners, frequently following them from room to room just to be near. Once in a great while they will speak, but only if they have something really important to say.

Temperamentally, Russian blues range from slightly aloof to charmingly shy. They demonstrate caution around strangers, and prefer to investigate new people slowly and gradually. Though not especially demonstrative, they are easily hurt when ignored. If neglected or stressed over long periods, they may go quietly mad.

Scottish fold. After two decades of crossbreeding American and British shorthairs, the Scottish fold has emerged as a cat that seems to define the word "wistful." Its round-tipped ears fold tightly forward and down over a roughly spherical head. Its eyes are large, wide-spaced, and supremely expressive. Its whiskers curve forward from prominent whisker pads, while its mouth seems bent in a perpetual smile. All in all, the Scottish fold looks like a baby in a bonnet, just begging to be held, rocked, or otherwise dandled. Fortunately, they seem to enjoy such treatment.

Scottish folds may be either longhairs or shorthairs. The longhaired variety isn't quite as bouffant as a Persian, but the males tend to sport a handsome ruff and a plumelike tail. Both types exhibit a wide array of colors, ranging from pure white, black, blue, or red, to tabby, calico, and patched.

Their temperament parallels their appearance. Scottish folds are extremely sweet and gentle, fond of their owners, and reticent with their opinions. They love to play, though usually only if you're involved. They enjoy sleeping on or as near a lap as possible, often on their backs.

Zest for Life

At the opposite end of the spectrum are cats who live for dashing from one part of the house to another, knocking things off high places, and inventing armies out of scraps of paper. If you have the patience for this type of behavior, an active cat will supply you with endless amusement and an enormous repertoire of stories to tell when your mother calls to ask what's been going on and you don't want to divulge anything that might be used against you at a later date.

Be warned, however, that active cats are happiest in spacious environments. Spacious is a relative term, of course. Cats tend to be smaller than most humans, and what may seem cramped to you may be perfectly adequate for someone a tenth of your size. Even if you live in a studio apartment, a sensible array of shelves, nooks, and cubbyholes may offer Boots enough variety to satisfy his needs. Just be sure the good china is stored in a secure place, well beyond the reach of slippery paws. Better yet, give it away.

Himalayan/Kashmir. One doesn't usually associate long-haired cats with kamikaze behavior. But these daredevils are the result of years of crossbreeding luxurious Persians with insanely curious Siamese. The result is an large, elegant-looking cat with fire in its belly — an ideal pet for anyone who wants an opulent pet with an adventurous nature. Himalayans have pointed coats, like Siamese, whereas Kashmirs are solid, usually either chocolate or lilac. Both are easygoing, and cope quite well with busy households and plucky children.

Chartreux. Famous for its gray-blue woolly coat, copper eyes, and powerful build, the Chartreux is a French breed whose origin has been lost in the dust of time. Though massive, they have mild temperaments, smiling expressions, and tiny voices. Some Chartreux cannot even meow at all, though they all have a satisfying rumbling purr. Since they aren't especially vocal, Chartreux may be easy to ignore. Over time, however, they've learned to get their owners' attention by batting their heavy paws or butting their heads against a well-placed shin.

Chartreux have long served as work cats, quite handy additions to a farm. They are excellent hunters, and in domestic situations display far more interest in "killing" a toy than in simply wrestling or pouncing. They play in short, vigorous spurts, sleeping and relaxing the rest of the day. They love to jump and run, often bounding from one inaccessible place to another with surprising agility. Consequently, they really need room to run around. For the same reason, they make exceptional companions for children and large dogs.

Somali. Somalis, originally considered a long-haired variant of Abyssinian, are lithe, muscular animals with medium-length fur and bushy tails, like foxes. Their coats are ticked, usually ruddy or fawn colored, which tends to dramatize their exotic, feral appearance. The effect is tempered somewhat by thin lines of dark color around their eyes, as if — though wild — they are bound by rules of fashion.

Like their Abyssinian forebears, Somalis are inquisitive and extraordinarily clever. They bound out of bed each morning with a long list of things to accomplish: There are garbage cans to explore, doors to open, pens to fling around, and papers to chew. Since their energy never seems to flag, they should be given lots of room to run around in, an abundance of toys, and scads of personal attention. Somalis seem happiest living with another cat that can keep up with them. They are, however, very even-tempered, and can handle chaotic households as well as life with other animals.

Affection

Some cats are just so nice to come home to. They run to the door, eager for the chance to rub against your legs and offer solace after a long day at the office or a noxious meeting at the club. They listen to your complaints without demanding that you hear them out first, or presenting you with a laundry list of things to do before you get your coat off. If they could mix you a nice martini, they probably would.

You are the center of their world. They are sensitive to your moods, and though they may feel a little lonely if you crave solitude or human company for a while, they generally won't hold it against you, or throw it in your face. In times of trouble or distress, the wordless comfort they offer — be it a warm paw wrapped around your neck or a few licks with a sandpapery tongue — can offer more real condolence than a stack of Hallmark cards.

Colorpoint shorthair. Half-sisters of the Siamese, Colorpoint shorthairs demonstrate the sterling combination of personal charm and svelte, stylish appearance. They are distinguished from their more famous relatives by a wider variety of point colors, including red, cream, several varieties of tortoise-point, and several more of lynx point.

Yet what really sets them apart is their intense need to love and be loved. They are enormously sensitive to the slightest shift in their owners' moods, and can be counted on to provide comfort, encouragement, and usually quite pertinent advice. They enjoy cuddling and sleeping on laps or riding on shoulders for a quick trip to the laundry room. In addition, whereas Siamese tend to devote their lives to one member of the household, Colorpoints are known to spread their affection equally among all members of the household — dogs, rabbits, ducks, and crotchety uncles included.

Havana brown. It has been observed that one does not own a Havana brown, but is owned by her. This is a cat who demands intimacy — not in an ugly or intrusive way, but in the manner of someone who has been through a lot of therapy, and doesn't see the point of coexisting with anyone on a superficial or neurotic level. She'll want to perch on your shoulders while you read the paper, sit beside you while you balance the checkbook, and sleep face-to-face with you in bed at night.

She can accept your needs, though. While you're off doing whatever it is you do with your special human friend, she can amuse herself with a paper bag, a cardboard box, or another cat.

When you return, she'll likely greet you with an outstretched paw; unlike most other cats, who typically rely on their noses for initial contact or investigation, a Havana brown prefers to touch first and ask questions later.

The coat of a Havana brown is a glossy, thick mahogany color. Some people believe the breed was named after the rabbit of the same hue, while others insist its name stems from a similarity to Havana cigars. The dispute will not likely be settled in our lifetime. In any case, a typical Havana brown has bright green, oval-shaped eyes, set lower in the face than those of other breeds; large, alertly poised ears; and a protruding, somewhat boxy muzzle. It is a distinct combination of features no other cat has been able to copy.

Chattiness

A variation on the affectionate cat is the happy talker. For people who live alone, or who have discovered to their horror that cable television merely offers seventy-plus variations on a theme of nothing to watch, a lively, chatty cat may be just the answer. His vocabulary is easily as large, if not larger, than the average teenager's, with the added advantage that most of what he has to say is pleasant.

In general, these cats are not well suited to people who work at home or enjoy immersing themselves in a good book: What at first seems a perfectly charming trait can quickly become annoying. If your mood tends toward the Brontë-esque, however, a furry raconteur may help lift you out of the moors and into a sunnier realm. Their attitude toward their owners has something of a grandmotherly quality — light, persistent, and genuinely caring.

Oriental shorthair. Orientals are a diverse group, ultimately derived from the Siamese. They are small and sleek, gliding across the room on tall, slender legs the envy of any would-be Giselle. Their nearly triangular heads are topped with large, flaring ears; their eyes, like those of their ancestors, are almond-shaped, but tend to be emerald green rather than blue. Don't let their svelte appearance fool you, though. These cats are heavier than they look, but it's all muscle.

Like roses, Orientals have been crossbred with an eye to developing new colors and patterns. Today, more than three hundred different variations are available, so you can pretty much count on finding an Oriental to coordinate even the most abstruse decor. Would you like a pure lavender cat? How about cinnamon with an undercoat of silver, or cream with tips of blue? Add a few red, brown, or smoke-gray stripes, and you have a lean, classy-looking tabby.

The personality of the Oriental shorthair is no less colorful and vibrant. These cats assume you've chosen them to share all the minute details of your life, so they make no bones whatsoever about participating in all your activities. A word or two while you're on the phone, a bit of advice with your wardrobe in the morning, and a running commentary on your cooking. If you return their attention and affection, they'll do just about anything to please you; these charming animals remain playful, spirited, and loyal long after their youth has flown. Ignore them, and they'll turn cranky, and probably start complaining about shooting pains in their hip or the noise from the stereo in the apartment next door.

Japanese bobtail. The Japanese bobtail is an ancient breed whose likeness has been rendered in paintings and carvings many centuries old. Statues of bobtails with one paw raised are considered good-luck charms, often placed prominently in storefronts and restaurants throughout Japan and other parts of Southeast Asia.

Japanese bobtails have small or medium builds. Their trademark feature is a stumpy tail covered in thick fur. It looks like a pompom, though it's probably not nice to mention the fact directly to the cat. Although bred in a variety of colors, the most popular bobtail seems to be the red, black, and white calico strain, known as *mi-ke*, or "three fur."

Graceful, energetic, and strong-willed, Japanese bobtails like to take charge of their families. Since they are not easily intimidated, they make excellent companions for children. For the same reason, though, you may find it difficult to dissuade them from doing something naughty, as they will quickly become indifferent to blasts of a squirt bottle, or any other method of negative reinforcement.

Companionship of some sort — human, feline, or otherwise — is essential to these cats; loneliness and boredom can lead to hooliganism. However, they are excellent conversationalists, with bright, chirpy little voices. They will often hum for their owners, which makes an attractive alternative to listening to the radio. And if you're really attentive, they'll even frolic around in a tub of water — a feat most other cats abhor.

Self-Reliance

Since most cats require less care than other types of pets, they are fast becoming the companion of choice for busy people, single people, and people who don't enjoy short trips to the fire hydrant in subzero weather. Yet, despite their reputation for independence, cats usually crave some form of companionship. Bereft of society, they are apt to become destructive, surly, or bizarrely religious.

Fortunately for those who would enjoy the company of a cat, but whose schedules require long hours away from home or frequent travel, certain breeds have demonstrated an ability to cope with solitude over extended periods; in former lives, they were probably renunciants. Of course, there is a trade-off for the convenience of owning a self-reliant cat. You can't expect him to come running every time you want company, or show off for the neighbors, or greet your guests at the door. Still, if you value your independence and would like to share your life with someone of equal temper, one of the following breeds may be just what you're looking for.

American wirehair. The American wirehair first appeared as a spontaneous mutation in a litter of farm cats in upstate New York. Though rare, such spontaneous appearances are not unheard of; however, this particular mutation seems to have occurred only in the United States. American wirehairs look as if they've accidentally stuck their paws in an electric socket. Their coat is coarse, crimped, and springy from ear to toe. Even their whiskers have a bit of a curl. More than thirty color variations are currently known, including solids, calico, and tortoiseshell patterns.

Despite their peculiar heritage, wirehairs don't seem to display any genetic weaknesses. They enjoy good health and sound tempers, are extremely easy to care for, and though friendly to their owners, tend to be somewhat more reserved around strangers than your typical American shorthair. However, because their coats can be easily damaged, they should never be brushed or combed. Bathing is the best way to deal with occasional deposits of lint or dust.

British shorthair. By all accounts the oldest English breed of cat, British shorthairs can trace their ancestry all the way back to the domestic cats of ancient Rome. While this may not seem especially significant to the larger population, British cats, like their human counterparts, tend to put a premium on family history. Initially recognized for their physical strength and hunting ability (another British obsession), shorthairs soon developed a reputation for endurance, loyalty, and grace under pressure.

Because of their calm demeanor and no-nonsense attitude, shorthairs are a favorite among animal trainers, often landing plum roles in films and television commercials. They tend to be reserved, watching the world roll by while occasionally letting fall a wry comment or two on the fallibility of conditioned existence. Once adopted into a family, they are devoted and undemanding companions.

Egyptian mau. Much to the chagrin of British shorthairs, maus can trace their ancestry at least as far back as 1400 B.C. Numerous documents and temple paintings from this period attest to the high degree of respect and worship accorded these handsome creatures. Descendants of the *Felis libyca* who long ago rid Egyptian granaries of rodents, maus are the only naturally spotted breed of domestic feline. Their base coat may be either silver, bronze, smoke, or black. Typically, dark lines on the forehead form an M — or scarab — pattern, while similar markings ring their gray-green eyes.

Maus are extremely intelligent and fiercely loyal. Supremely conscious of their divine history, they often appear aloof; most do not usually enjoy being picked up or handled. They are moderately active, preferring to prowl between the sofa and the magazine rack, rather than chase a casually tossed toy. When amused or happy, they tend to chortle softly, and wag their tails rapidly while treading the rug with their forepaws.

Cats That Act Like Dogs (Only Better)

"A cat is not a dog," according to T. S. Eliot. Any cat will tell you the same thing — adding, perhaps, that while dogs may have much to recommend them, they are not, and never will be, cats. Still, people persist in wanting dogs.

Devotion seems to be one of the most appealing qualities dogs have to offer their owners. Like humans and other primates, dogs are pack animals. The strongest and wisest animal stands at the top of the social ladder, with the rest arranged on lower rungs according to their lights. Since allegiance to one's superiors is the code of canine society, domesticated dogs gallantly (if not always wisely) tender their whole hearts to their human keepers. They may make mistakes now and again, but their love is true and pure.

Alas, the same cannot always be said of cats. Cats live to please themselves, and insofar as you please them, they will make good efforts to ensure a steady supply of companionship and warmth. Yet some among this clever breed do seem capable of devotion above and beyond their nature. They speak, they sit, they come when called. They demonstrate an investment in their owner's life, not for any potential gain, but strictly for its own sake.

Add to this special type of devotion all the other advantages of cat ownership, and you have a nearly perfect companion who doesn't slobber and won't eat your couch.

American shorthair. Perhaps the most well-known variety of cat, this happy breed is typically pictured in children's alphabet books under the title "C Is for Cat" Do not, however, confuse familiarity with mediocrity. Though American shorthairs may jump through hoops in television commercials, pose for calendars, and happily endorse a wide array of cat foods, there is nothing common about them. In fact, there are more than thirty pedigreed varieties of American shorthairs, each distinguished by color and pattern; probably the most familiar patterns are tabby, calico, and tortoiseshell. Nonpedigreed shorthairs, meanwhile, may display any number of colors and patterns.

Probably because their ancestry is a somewhat mixed affair, American shorthairs are known for their even disposition and general good health. They have strong bodies and clever minds, enabling them to adapt to just about any living situation. Though they enjoy company, their lives don't depend on endless parties, lavish praise, or expensive gifts. A lump of food, a bowl of water, and thou — that's all it takes to keep them happy.

One notable feature common to all American shorthairs is their exceptional hunting ability. They make excellent mousers, though in the absence of a distinguishable rodent population, they will handily rid your home of other pests, such as flies, spiders, and roaches. Really, they'll chase whatever moves, and if it doesn't put up too much of a fight, they'll probably eat it, too. If your home is pest-free, you may have to provide stimulation on your own; otherwise Buster may begin to lean toward the heavy side.

One of the nicest parts about owning this type of cat, actually, is that they do enjoy a good wrestling match or race down the hallway. They even can tolerate rough or clumsy handling from well-meaning children. In fact, American shorthairs become quite attached to their families — often running to the door when they hear the key, and answering when called.

Maine coon. "Delicate" is perhaps not the first word that springs to mind in describing this strong, confident long-haired cat. Maine coons can weigh anywhere between twelve and eighteen pounds, and their heavy, tufted coats make them wonderful bedfellows for cold winter nights. Despite their size, they have tiny voices, tending to communicate by means of high-pitched squeaks, chirps, and trills.

Rumor has it that Maine coons came to North America on the earliest European sailing vessels, and adapted to the harsh conditions of New England colonial life as readily as the staunchest Puritans. They display no prudish tendencies, however, and have never been known to impose their beliefs on their neighbors. On the contrary, Maine coons are wonderfully tolerant, adore large families, and like to take charge of chaotic situations.

Ocicat. Ocicats are spotted cats, though unlike maus, they have not come by their spots naturally, but rather through selective breeding. They are strong, athletic animals with long tails and moderately large ears. The females tend to be smaller than the males, but both sexes enjoy leaping, pouncing, and other vigorous pursuits.

Ocicats may look dangerous, but their temperament is pure puppy. As a rule, Ocicats do not see people, just new laps to sit in. Of course, should a lap not be available, a cozy pair of shoulders will do. The view is nice, and it's fun to ride from room to room around the house like a Raj atop an elephant. When the elephant gets tired of carrying them, they don't mind simply following along behind. People who own Ocicats often feel as though they've acquired an extra shadow.

Ocicats are highly intelligent, and a joy to train. Many will fetch, walk on a leash, respond to commands, and submit to all manner of household rules. Those who learn to travel early on also make ideal companions for a long trip or vacation; they look forward to the trip, and generally won't need to hang their heads out the car window. Breezy, charming, and socially outgoing, they don't like being left alone for long periods; by the same token, they adapt quite handily to busy, crowded households.

Distinctive Looks

Most people have a fairly fixed idea of what a cat should look like. The prototypical cat is furry and warm, has long whiskers and a proud tail, and is fairly nice to hold in one's lap. Real style is much more a matter of character than expectation, though. It takes a certain amount of pluck to defy convention and express one's real nature. Though the world may not approve, maturity is often most reliably defined by the volume of dissent aimed in one's direction.

If you're looking for an animal of distinction, and aren't afraid of criticism, you might want to consider one of these charming and highly unusual breeds.

Cornish Rex. The Cornish Rex is a slim, smallish cat with an arched body, long legs, and an oval-shaped head. It has a fine, aristocratic profile, comprised of a tapered muzzle, a high forehead, and a rather aquiline nose. Its graceful neck and high cheekbones enhance the effect of sophisticated elegance. Yet what truly distinguishes this breed from the rest is its coat. The short, silky hairs lie close to the skin in neatly marcelled waves.

No amount of paper curls or patient hours under the hair dryer can reproduce these fine ripples. Like the American wirehair, this cat is a genetic mutation. All present-day Cornish Rex are descended from a single cat, born in a litter of barn cats in Cornwall in 1950. A wide range of colors are available to suit the strangest fancy. You can find solid Rex, bicolored, calico, and striped; some varieties even display the distinctive point patterns common to the Siamese.

While enormously agile and extroverted, Cornish Rex are equally affectionate cuddlers. They are just as happy playing games as sitting in their owners' laps. Unfortunately, they are so odd-looking, not everyone will want to hold them. Cornish Rex are perhaps best suited to people with modern tastes. However, because their hair is so fine and short, they seem to be less likely to provoke allergic responses in people allergic to other types of cats.

Manx/Cymric. A number of mythical tales surround the origins of the Manx. Perhaps the most famous is the one that has Noah shutting the door rather hastily on its tail just as the rain began to fall. In fact, the Manx originated on the Isle of Man, off the coast of Great Britain. Centuries ago, a spontaneous mutation produced a litter of kittens born without the vertebrae that form the tail. Because the isolation of their native land inhibited opportunities for outside breeding, taillessness eventually became the Manx's dominant trait.

Manx are stocky, solidly built cats, with thick double coats, broad chests, and arched backs. Their heads are quite round, set with fat, jowly whisker pads; the males, especially, tend to look like Winston Churchill in his later years. Three varieties of taillessness are traditionally observed. "Rumpies" have a dimple where the tail should be; "stumpies" have a small piece of cartilage extending from the base of the spine; and "longies" — the black sheep of the Manx family — actually sport tails. Only rumpies are considered show-quality cats.

Manx have been bred in a variety of colors, and may be either long-haired or short-haired. Long-haired Manx are often known as Cymrics — a Welsh word you may only have heard if you've ever had the misfortune of attending a Renaissance festival; it simply means Celtic. Cymrics resemble Manx in every way, except for a thicker coat and a broad ruff beneath the chin. Both types are quiet, even-tempered animals that don't tend to rush into close relationships with their owners. Once a bond is forged, though, it's virtually indestructible.

They can also become extremely protective of their homes. An odd noise or disturbance can provoke a low growl from a Manx, while an intruder may be attacked with surprising ferocity. Nevertheless, a young Manx can learn to tolerate rambunctious children. An older animal may have a harder time adapting to all the noise and sudden movements.

A word of caution: The gene that causes taillessness can produce a special medical problem known as Manx Syndrome.

Occasionally, a kitten's spine may be shortened too far, resulting in defects such as a gap in the last few vertebrae, fused vertebrae, or deformed spines. The problem may not be obvious at birth; difficulties usually arise in the first few weeks, though sometimes as late as four months. They are usually characterized by severe bowel and/or bladder dysfunction, or by extreme difficulty in walking.

Sphynx. Stranger than a curly cat, and far more rare than a tailless cat, the Sphynx is completely, undeniably bald. The typical response to this exotic creature is either laughter or revulsion. It takes a certain innocence of eye to recognize their unusual beauty, and a certain sensitivity of touch to appreciate their fine, leathery skin. Sphynx have remarkably sweet expressions, accented by huge ears that seem to dwarf their tiny faces. They are the most affectionate cats known to man, constantly purring, and craving physical contact.

Sphynx are lean animals, blessed with high metabolisms. Though they require frequent feeding, you'd be hard put to find a fat Sphynx. Their skin tends to exude oil, so they do require regular bathing; they should never be left to air-dry, however. In fact, since these animals are extremely sensitive to cold, and only develop a sparse down in winter, care should be taken to ensure they are kept warm at all times of the year. This is one cat who doesn't mind being dressed in funny little sweaters.

A Summary of Breeds

Generally speaking, visual aids serve two related purposes. In the first place, they organize complex information for easy reference. Secondly, and perhaps more importantly, they relieve the tedium often induced by reading.

It is fervently hoped the following charts will facilitate the process of choosing the cat most likely to suit your needs. Several categories are offered for consideration, including body type, personality, compatibility, and activity level. You will no doubt observe that long-haired and short-haired breeds have been assigned to separate charts. This arrangement does not reflect personal or historical prejudices of any kind; it is intended purely for convenience, since longhairs in general require a higher degree of maintenance than shorthairs. A more complete discussion of feline grooming can be found in Chapter Five.

Finally, those breeds that have not been described in detail above are marked with an asterisk.

Breed	Description	Size	Temperament	Compatibility	Activity Level
LONG-HAIRED CATS					
American Curl	Thick, powerful body with semilong to long coat. Available in a wide variety of colors and patterns. Distinguished by the ears, which are firm, round, and curl gracefully back away from the face.	L	Curious, playful, loving, doglike, independent	C, P	Moderate
Balinese	Elegant. Medium-length, silky coat. Traditional Siamese points. Blue eyes.	M	Curious, playful, loving, vocal	C, V	Active
Birman	Fluffy, long coat. Pointed, with golden tinge. White paws. Blue, penetrating eyes. Regal.	L	Playful, independent	C, V	Placid
Cymric	Long-haired variant of Manx. Tailless. Moderately long coat with broad ruff. A wide variety of colors.	L	Curious, loving, doglike	C, P, V	Moderate
Himalayan	Thick body. Long, fine coat. Pointed. Blue eyes.	L	Curious, playful, loving, doglike, vocal	C, P, V	Active
Javanese	Like Balinese, with wider variety of point colors.	M	Curious, playful, loving, vocal	C, V	Active

Breed	Description	Size	Temperament	Compatibility	Activity Level
Kashmir	Like Himalayan, except solid-colored. Chocolate or lilac.	L	Curious, playful, loving, doglike, vocal	C, P, V	Active
Maine coon	Shaggy, double coat with extremely fluffy tail. Wide variety of colors and patterns, but the most common is brown tabby.	L	Curious, loving, doglike	C, P, V	Moderate
Nebelung	A long-haired variant of the Russian blue. Slender, with a medium-long, silky blue coat.	M	Loving, doglike	C, P	Placid
Norwegian forest cat	Long, rich fur with thick undercoat. Flowing tail. Powerful build. Fast, smart, and courageous. A hardy animal.	L	Curious, loving, doglike	C, P, V	Active
Oriental longhair	A long-haired variant of the Oriental short-hair. Sleek, muscular, nearly triangular head. Variety of colors and patterns.	S	Curious, playful, loving, doglike, vocal	C, V	Active

KEY: CHILDREN–C, OTHER PETS–P, VISITORS–V

Breed	Description	Size	Temperament	Compatibility	Activity Level
Persian	Broad, chunky body. Luxurious coat. Round, massive head, flat nose, and tiny ears. Wide, expressive eyes. Huge variety of colors and patterns.	L	Curious, loving, doglike	P	Placid
Ragdoll	Thick, pointed coat with white mittens. Broad ruff and a long tail. Long nose and blue eyes. Famous for its sweet, docile nature.	L	Playful, loving, doglike	C, P, V	Moderate
Somali	Lithe body. Medium-long coat with fluffy tail and hindquarters. Ruddy or red, with gold or green eyes. Looks like a fox, and just as smart.	M	Curious, playful, loving, doglike	C, P, V	Active
Tiffany	Long-haired variant of Burmese. Solid body, with long, silky hair. Very fluffy neck fur. Wide, round eyes and tiny ears. Sable-colored, with lighter tips. A charmer. Also known as "Chantilly."	M	Playful, loving, doglike, vocal	C, V	Active

Breed	Description	Size	Temperament	Compatibility	Activity Level
Turkish Angora	Graceful, lithe body. Medium-long, glossy coat. Long, full tail usually carried quite high. Extremely fastidious; likes to play in water. Highly intelligent. Easily trained to perform tricks. Usually white with blue eyes, though other colors are becoming popular.	S	Playful, loving, doglike	C	Moderate
Turkish Van	White, semilong fur with auburn coloration restricted to head and tail. Coat is waterproof and has cashmerelike texture. Loves water. Very intelligent and brave. Doesn't mind going for walks.	L	Playful, loving, doglike, independent	P	Moderate
Short-Haired Cats					
Abyssinian	Lithe, fast, fearless. Short, ticked coat. Ruddy or red. Looks like a small mountain lion. Loves high places.	S	Curious, playful, loving, doglike, vocal	C, P, V	Active

KEY: CHILDREN-C, OTHER PETS-P, VISITORS-V

85

Breed	Description	Size	Temperament	Compatibility	Activity Level
American shorthair	Powerful, usually heavy build. Open, sweet face. Generally good-natured, but much depends on family history. Males can be quite a bit larger than females. Pedigrees come in 30+ colors and patterns; infinite variety in nonpedigreed cats. Also called "Domestic shorthair."	M, L	Curious, playful, loving, independent	C, P, V	Moderate
American wirehair	Muscular build, round head, like American shorthair. Distinguished by its springy, crimped coat and whiskers.	M	Loving, independent	C, P	Moderate
Bombay	Jet-black with round, coppery eyes. Incredibly muscular body and round head. Males may be quite a bit bigger than females. Gorgeous and easygoing. Likes to perform.	M, L	Playful, loving	C, P, V	Active
British shorthair	Massive, stocky, and round. Has been called "a ball in a box." Reserved and unflappable.	L	Loving, independent	C, P, V	Placid

Breed	Description	Size	Temperament	Compatibility	Activity Level
Bengal	Exotic, relatively new crossbreed of wild Asian leopard cats and domestic shorthairs. A powerful, spotted cat with a glossy coat. Intelligent and very active. May display wild tendencies of its forebears.	L	Curious, playful, independent		Active
Burmese	Compact, muscular, with round head and small ears. Short, glossy, deep brown coat. Round eyes. Lives for applause.	M	Curious, playful, loving, doglike, vocal	C, P, V	Active
Chartreux	Big, friendly cat with a woolly blue coat and orange eyes. Famous for its smiling expression. A terrific mouser.	L	Curious, loving, doglike, independent	C, P	Active
Colorpoint shorthair	Lean, very dainty build. Short coat and fine bones. Blue eyes. A variety of point colors. Unusually devoted and sensitive to moods.	S	Curious, playful, loving, doglike, vocal	C, P, V	Active
Cornish Rex	Very stylish-looking. Long, lithe body, with narrow head, whiplike tail, and enormous ears. Velvety fur full of tight, close waves. A lap cat for the connoisseur.	S	Playful, loving, vocal	C, P, V	Moderate

KEY : CHILDREN–C, OTHER PETS–P, VISITORS–V

Breed	Description	Size	Temperament	Compatibility	Activity Level
Devon Rex	Similar to a Cornish Rex, but with longer, fuzzier coat. Body type more finely sculptured, not as extreme. Very sensitive to cold and heat.	S	Curious, playful, loving, doglike	V	Moderate
Egyptian mau	Naturally spotted coat; base is either silver, bronze, or smoke. Gray–green eyes. Very reserved and supremely graceful.	M	Curious, independent		Moderate
Exotic shorthair	A short-haired Persian. Stocky body, round head and eyes. Puffy cheeks and short nose. Thick, plush coat. Sweet and undemanding.	L	Playful, loving, independent	C	Placid
Havana brown	Bulging, boxy muzzle. Long legs. Warm brown coat and whiskers. Vivid green eyes. Loves to be around people. Hates being left alone. Will greet you with outstretched paw.	M	Curious, playful, loving, doglike, vocal	C, P, V	Active
Japanese bobtail	Short, puffy bunny tail. Muscular, lean body. Many patterns available, though most common is white with red and black markings (considered good luck). Enjoys taking charge.	M	Playful, loving, doglike, vocal	C, P, V	Moderate

Breed	Description	Size	Temperament	Compatibility	Activity Level
Korat	Heart-shaped face. Silver-blue coat with silver tips. Wide green or amber eyes. Dignified and responsible. Will often alert owners to intruders and other emergencies.	M	Loving, doglike, independent	C	Active
Malayan	A variant of Burmese. Blue, tawny, or platinum coat. Wide, round eyes. Inquisitive and very playful.	M	Curious, playful, loving, doglike, vocal	C, P, V	Active
Manx	Tailless. Surprisingly heavy for its size. Thick double coat requires frequent brushing. A bit devilish, but devoted. Good watchcat.	M	Curious, playful, loving, doglike	C, P	Moderate
Ocicat	Spotted pattern and various color backgrounds. Lean, powerful build. Dramatically beautiful, looks like a wildcat. Males can grow a good deal larger than females.	M, L	Curious, loving, doglike		Placid
Oriental shorthair	Small and svelte, like a Siamese. Huge ears and triangular faces. A variety of colors and patterns. Most have green eyes; whites usually have blue eyes. Very devoted.	S	Curious, playful, loving, doglike, vocal	C, P, V	Active

KEY : CHILDREN–C, OTHER PETS–P, VISITORS–V

Breed	Description	Size	Temperament	Compatibility	Activity Level
Russian blue	Short, plush, silvery-blue coat. Green eyes. Lithe body and long legs. Very gentle and devoted to owners.	M	Loving, doglike, independent	C, P	Placid
Scottish fold	Folded ears and wide face, and big, round eyes give a wistful impression. Prominent whisker pads. Stocky body and dense coat. A wide variety of colors and patterns. Needs constant cuddling and reassurance.	M	Curious, loving, doglike	C, P	Placid
Siamese	Amazingly long and thin. Fine, pointed coat. Big ears, blue eyes. Perhaps the most intelligent, curious, talkative breed. Loyal, fearless, and willful. Tends to be devoted to one person.	S	Curious, playful, loving, doglike, vocal	C	Active
Singapura	Tiny, with wide, expressive eyes. Warm beige, ticked coat. Silky. Aggressively affectionate, and rarely disagreeable.	S	Curious, playful, loving, doglike	C, V	Moderate

Breed	Description	Size	Temperament	Compatibility	Activity Level
Snowshoe	A hybrid of American shorthair and Siamese. Hefty, big ears. Pointed coat with unusual white chest, mask, and feet. Very sweet and devoted.	M	Loving, doglike	C, P	Moderate
Sphynx	Completely bald, except for nearly invisible down in winter. Leathery, wrinkled skin feels warm and slightly oily. Sculpted body like a Rex. Wide variety of colors and patterns, which, in the absence of fur, look like tattoos. Extremely affectionate. Sensitive to cold.	M	Curious, loving, doglike, vocal	C, P	Moderate
Tonkinese	Hybrid of Burmese and Siamese. Short, glossy coat feels like mink. Pointed, but point color is not contrasting, but rather a deeper shade of base coat. Aqua eyes.	M	Curious, playful, loving, doglike, vocal	C, P, V	Active

KEY : CHILDREN–C, OTHER PETS–P, VISITORS–V

CHAPTER 4

"Your" Home Is "Our" Home

It would be nice to say that the clitter-clatter of little claws across the hardwood floor is always the end result of careful deliberation. Often, however, cat adoption is more of an impromptu affair. You pass a store window and your heart turns to pudding, or your child or your partner is suddenly stricken with a kind of hunger that cannot be assuaged by an ice-cream cone. Sometimes the cat simply appears, either on your doorstep, or in the beam of your car headlights, or crawling bedraggled and terrified from an alley.

Regardless of the manner of your cat's arrival, the next step is fairly predictable. You'll need to make a few adjustments to your home. These aren't necessarily expensive or strenuous; the most challenging task of all is probably psychological. Caring for a small, somewhat wily, dependent creature requires common sense — a type of mindfulness not generally associated with everyday living. Yet perhaps this shift in mental attitude is the true motive behind feline adoption. Under all the sales talk about life being fast, fun, and odor-free, may burn an awareness that a cat can relieve you of the terrible burden of self-interest.

Any physical adjustments you need to make will typically fall under one of the following categories:

- Taste

- Safety

- Convenience

Taste, in this instance, involves specifically feline values; it is assumed you have already defined and provided for your own. Likewise, safety refers to measures taken to protect your cat, not yourself or your possessions, from tragic misadventures. However, in order to create a mutually satisfying environment, you and your cat may have to negotiate certain demands in both areas. Any and all such discussions are perhaps best understood as issues of convenience.

SHARING THE TERRITORY

One of the most profound, though subtle, changes that occurs upon introducing a cat into your environment is a redefinition of the space itself. Formerly, it was your "home"; now it is his "territory." It may take a while to notice this transformation, since your cat will probably spend his first few days making a thorough investigation of the place (a process explored in more detail in Chapter Five). When you catch him sprawled out comfortably somewhere, and he doesn't immediately sit up or bolt like a guilty schoolboy, you'll know he's taken the measure of his kingdom and found it very good.

Once he's comfortable, he'll probably choose several spots for reclining. These are his thrones, and generally he won't like to share them. Fortunately, most will be situated where other members of the household rarely tread: perhaps on a windowsill or the top of the refrigerator. By day, he may curl up on the bed, since you won't be using it; in the evening, he might prefer the ugly chair in the living room that no one likes to sit in, but which gives him a fairly panoramic view of human activity. Like any human ruler, a cat knows that a kingdom is a sometime thing: Successful stewardship depends on constant vigilance.

From a feline point of view, just about any type of home makes an interesting territory. To him, his mere presence makes it so. Still, a little attention to details can ensure that he finds his new home particularly stimulating. And if he's truly content, chances are you will enjoy sharing the space all the more.

Size of Space

Though it seems to create all manner of psychological hardships for human beings, the whole issue of size doesn't matter to a cat. In almost all cases, variety makes a much more important contribution to well-being. The only exception might be a highly active cat. Yet even a Chartreux or Somali can find happiness in small quarters, so long as the furnishings are arranged with an eye to leaping, galloping, and other expressions of athletic prowess.

Studio Apartments. Unless you're only eighteen inches tall and weigh somewhere in the vicinity of fifteen pounds, chances are you haven't even begun to explore the possibilities of a one-room apartment. You probably take it for granted that there's only so much you can do to accommodate your needs and tastes. A pleasant surprise awaits you, then, when you introduce a cat into your home, for he will discover therein a variety and complexity you could not have imagined.

For example, that space between the couch and the chest of drawers behind it turns out to be a cave. Maybe you've stuffed the polyester afghan you inherited from Aunt Margaret back there; now it's a cave with a comfortable lining. The top of your computer monitor or television set makes a nice, warm perch (especially convenient if you're sitting captive in front of it). On hot summer days, the porcelain hollow of a bathroom sink can be a cool spot to while away an hour. A table draped with a nice long cloth, meanwhile, provides the perfect setting for one of your cat's favorite games: "If I Don't See You, You Don't Exist."

A little imagination can go a long way in making a small apartment more attractive to a cat. Clear a space on the windowsill, where he can relax in the sun and watch the busy traffic of all the little people out there in the street. Likewise, you might reserve a place for perching on top of a dresser; it's as good an excuse as any to get rid of knicknacks you've come to regret. You could nail a couple of shelves to the wall, placed at different heights, so Buster can step or leap comfortably from one to the other.

If you're not particularly handy, or if the landlord frowns on additions of this sort, you might consider investing in a climbing tree (basically, a series of shelves attached at different heights to a central post). Climbing trees are available in a variety of styles and sizes from most pet shops and some large discount stores. Most climbing trees are small enough that you can move them around the apartment if the mood strikes you, or you acquire a new piece of furniture.

Finally, if it's at all possible, you might want to leave some sort of unobstructed path for a quiet stroll or a hearty gallop. Even placid cats occasionally like to run, and it's no fun to bump into furniture at full tilt. You may find that not having to negotiate an obstacle course from the front door to the stereo contributes to your own peace of mind, as well.

Larger Abodes. Naturally, life in a place that has more than one room offers considerably more stimulation for a cat. There are simply more areas to explore and exploit. A larger living space also reduces the likelihood that you and your cat will get annoyed with each other's presence. Disconcerting as it may be, cats, like people, sometimes go through periods where they just don't want to deal with intrusions of any kind — no matter how charming and attractive said intrusion may be.

Still, even in a multiroom dwelling, it's a good idea to make some special provision for your cat's aesthetic priorities. You can live in Buckingham Palace, but if every nightstand and end table is cluttered with photos, figurines, and other sentimental curios, Misty may feel — justifiably — denied her due. If the condition persists, she may take matters into her own paws, as it were, and clear a perch or two for herself.

Doors are another source of potential conflict. Like their wild forebears, domestic cats are compelled by nature to make several tours of their territory each day, just to make sure everything is in order and properly scented. A closed door presents a disagreeable impediment to the call of nature.

Some of the more cunning and imaginative breeds, like Siamese or Abyssinian, can learn to manipulate doorknobs and handles, resolving the dilemma with surprising ingenuity. Most others fall back on more primitive but ultimately no less successful methods. Typically, they will sit in front of the closed door meowing, or scratching, or both. It is wise not to underestimate the tenacity of a cat who knows what he wants. Unlike people, who can to some degree defer gratification and even enjoy fantasies of fulfillment, cats have no patience for anything beyond direct, immediate experience. In practical terms, this means that if your cat can smell you hiding behind your bedroom door, he will not cease from calling attention to himself until you let him in. On the other hand, if you have simply closed the door (whether purposely or absentmindedly), he will eventually give up, but probably not before leaving a few claw marks on the door. Though to you this may seem like a destructive move, to the cat it more or less serves as a reminder to all comers that whatever lies behind the door is his, and woe betide whoever dares lay claim to it.

One door in particular must never be closed: The room, or closet, or cubbyhole where the litter box has been established must remain accessible at all times. To block entry to this area is to invite disaster of an unspeakable nature.

A Room of One's Own

In general, cats living in a multiroom dwelling do not enjoy being confined to a single room like the first Mrs. Rochester in *Jane Eyre*. They imagine wonders on the other side of the door, and sooner or later their need to explore will overcome them. In an excited state, cats can move very fast; before you can respond, they're off and running.

Some cats can be trained to spend the night in a closed-off area of the home. It is absolutely essential that the litter box occupy the same quarters, and ideally a bowl of water and a bit of food. A toy or two might help to pass the long hours away from you. Even so, you may have to put up with a few nights of hapless meowing before Matilda realizes that she's on her own for the night.

However, if crying or destructive behavior persists for more than a week, you may need to reconsider your plan. If your cat's nocturnal prowling has forced you to close her up for the night, try feeding her just before bedtime. Cats are usually most relaxed and sleepy after meals. If you simply don't care for the idea of sharing your bed with a warm, furry creature who wants nothing more than to be with you, you might try establishing a special place for her to sleep — either in your bedroom or some other area of the house.

Most cats like to retreat to some sort of den for part of the day. It needn't be elaborate or situated in an isolated place. More than likely, your cat will have already discovered for herself certain hiding spots for those times when she really wants to be alone. A den, by contrast, is usually a confined or protected space and thus affords an opportunity to sit up and take stock of the entire room every now and then. Its appeal lies in the ability to enjoy some sense of privacy in public.

A den can be a cardboard box, a paper bag, an open closet, or even an empty wastebasket. If you really want your cat to be committed to his den, you should let him choose it. Holidays, birthdays, and other gift-giving occasions provide especially auspicious opportunities for choosing a den. After you've unwrapped your cheese and sausage gift crate or a year's supply of Great-aunt Ida's fruitcake, Mr. Buttons may wander over to the empty box and impulsively leap inside. If he stays there till the aroma of roasting goose becomes too tempting, you can safely say he's found his den.

A cat who has a den of his own will likely spend less time on the furniture, and more readily embrace the idea of not sleeping with you, than a cat who is not so fortunate. Most cat owners will gladly trade the relative inconvenience of an ugly box in the middle of the living room for a reprieve from vacuuming fifty pounds of cat hair off the sofa once or twice a week. If the den your cat has chosen is truly appalling to behold, you can try moving it to a less prominent area, or render its appearance more acceptable by painting the outside, or covering it with remainders or wrapping paper. The more ambitious may even try découpage, though the smell of varnish or polyurethane may deter your cat from resuming occupancy once the project is completed.

Beds, Bowls, and Beyond

While any number of specialty items are available on the market today, most seem designed to appeal to cat owners rather than to cats themselves. In general, the feline aesthetic does not run toward kitsch. When shopping for articles your cat will use on a daily basis, the main point to remember is practicality. A cunning kitty couch may fit comfortably in the context of your decorating scheme, but if kitty does not fit comfortably on the couch, it will fast become another piece of junk waiting around for the next garage sale. Nevertheless, a few articles should be on hand when your cat arrives.

Cat Beds. If you've ever spent a night at a motel or on a friend's foldout sofa, you've probably come to appreciate the fact that not all sleeping accommodations are alike. Personal idiosyncracies play a large role in choosing a comfortable mattress. What seems ideal to one person may feel like a bed of nails to another. There is no reason to assume that cats should experience things any differently.

True, most cats are covered in fur, which tends to cushion their bodies against the most unlikely surfaces. But just as you would probably think twice about curling up for a long winter's nap on a pile of old shoes, your cat may express certain reservations about occupying the miniature sleigh bed you've spent a small fortune on, thinking he'll look adorable sleeping in it.

It cannot be emphasized enough that a cat does not give a fig about how his bed looks. How it smells figures much more significantly. This is perhaps one of the main reasons why cats prefer sleeping with their owners rather than anywhere else; when sleeping, most people smell like animals. And unless you're given to a daily rotation of sheets, blankets, pillows, and quilts, your bedding is apt to retain a certain pungency long after you've risen, showered, and gone to work.

In the long run, your cat will probably choose his bed the same way he selects his den; in fact, the two may be considered synonymous. The ideal cat bed will offer a sense of privacy and protection, and at the same time exude a delicately "natural" odor that may or may not be discerned by the human nostril. It would be a nice gesture on your part to provide several alternatives before your cat arrives, so that he can choose the one he likes best. Not only will such an arrangement make your cat feel welcome, but it will also enable you to exercise some control over where he sleeps.

Bowls. Mealtime is probably the highlight of a cat's day. Because their focus is the food itself, most cats aren't concerned with the relative elegance or rudeness of their table setting. The critical factor is stability. When it comes to eating, all decorum is thrust aside, and even the most adept or sophisticated cat will dive face first into his food. A bowl that is likely to tip or slide across the floor as one probes its contents with one's nose can prove extremely frustrating.

For maximal dining comfort, dishes should be sturdy and nonsliding. A number of nice, heavy bowls with flat or rubber-tipped bottoms are available in pet stores, though baby food dishes may serve quite handily. For your own peace of mind, the sides of the food bowls should be a couple of inches tall, because bits of food tend to drop out of a cat's mouth as he feeds. A placemat or piece of newspaper set underneath the bowl will help contain crumbs and other evidence of inelegant dining habits, as well as minimize slipping and sliding.

Some people prefer using one bowl for dry food, and another for moist rations. This is a matter of personal taste, and no recommendation is offered in this volume. However, bowls in which moist food has been served should be washed once daily, as whatever remains in them quickly becomes crusty and malodorous. While this phenomenon will probably not offend your cat, you may not find it particularly inviting as you stumble into the kitchen to make the morning coffee.

A separate water bowl should be maintained at all times. Cats drink at various times during the day, and you can never predict when thirst will strike. Ideally, fresh water should be set out every day, and the bowl should be scrubbed and rinsed every couple of days, since sediment of various kinds tends to settle at the bottom.

The location of the feeding area is largely up to you. Obviously, it should be consistent and readily accessible: Consider how you would feel if you had to hunt out your dinner every single day of your life, or contort your body in order to eat under a cupboard. Most cat owners prefer to feed their pets in the kitchen, in order to facilitate cleanup.

Litter Boxes and Related Accessories. If you can only afford one specifically cat-oriented item, it must be a litter box. No other object can compare with its importance. Plastic is the preferred material, since it is light and fairly easy to clean. In a pinch, you can use an aluminum turkey roasting pan; but, since they are not as durable, they should only be reserved for emergency use.

You may choose between three basic types of litter box:

a. *A simple plastic pan*, between four and five inches tall and eighteen to twenty-four inches long, should provide ample room for your cat's private needs. A plastic dishpan of these proportions will serve. It's easily transportable, making it ideal for traveling.

b. *Plastic pans with detachable rims*, available at most pet shops and discount stores, can help prevent litter from scattering as your cat buries its waste and leaps from the pan.

c. *A litter box with a fitted domelike lid* can help control scattering, as well as contain odors and offer your cat a greater sense of privacy. Don't be lulled into a false sense of security concerning odors, however. While it may take a little longer for you to notice unpleasant smells emanating from a covered litter box, the ghastly aroma that gathers under the lid after a couple of days of neglect will make cleaning out waste all the more unpleasant.

In addition to the box itself, you will, of course, need litter. Bags and jugs of various sizes are available in pet stores and most supermarkets. You will need enough to fill the box to at least a two-inch depth, and more to maintain that level as you remove waste.

Litter comes in several different varieties:

a. *Clumping litter* is generally considered the easiest to manage. Urine trapped by the finely ground clay that is the basis of the litter forms handy clumps, reducing odor and allowing for easy removal. Very rarely are these clumps as perfectly spherical as they are often depicted in advertisements. Still, the convenience is appreciable.

b. *Nonclumping litter* is moderately less expensive, but does not usually trap urine as efficiently. Like the clumping variety, the base material consists of finely ground clay, which seems to be the toilet material of choice among domestic cats. Cats like to bury their waste, and ground clay is light enough to dig, yet solid enough to cover all manner of excreta.

c. *Chemically treated litter* contains perfumes, tracking and scattering inhibitors, and odor managers. It is not really wise to fill the cat box with chemically treated material. Cats inhale the dust from their litter, and lick off whatever material gets stuck between their toes. Though the proportion of chemical additives is fairly minimal, over time these can accrue in the cat's respiratory system or digestive tract, potentially leading to health problems.

d. *Non-clay-based litters* are fast becoming a popular alternative to traditional litters. Some of the more common varieties are made from peanut shells or cedar chips, and seem to be effective at controlling odors and reducing scattering and tracking. Not all cats will accept alternative varieties, however, so it's best to have some clay litter on hand, just in case Muffin decides your pillow would make a better comfort station than a box of ground-up peanut shells.

Finally, you will need a plastic or metal scoop to remove solid waste and urine clumps from the box. This duty should be performed once a day; more frequently if you have more than one cat or are particularly concerned about odors. Every couple of days you will need to add more litter, to make up for whatever you've discarded. Once a week — or at least once every two weeks — the entire box should be emptied and washed out with soap and hot water. Don't use ammonia, chlorine bleach, or heavily scented soaps, as strong chemical smells offend sensitive feline nostrils, and trace amounts adhering to the box may end up poisoning your cat. Lysol, in particular, is toxic to cats. Pregnant women should never handle soiled litter, which can harbor the parasite that causes toxoplasmosis. See Chapter Six for further discussion of this important subject.

While placement of the litter box is a matter of personal preference, three general rules obtain. First, as mentioned earlier, the box must be located in a consistently accessible location. Second, the location should be reasonably private and protected. Unlike dogs, cats prefer to go about their business unobserved, and if regularly interrupted, will probably choose an area that provides a greater sense of sanctity. Finally, the litter box should not be placed near your cat's feeding area. The reason for this is perhaps less obvious than it appears. Odors arising from feline waste mark the limits of a cat's territory, a sign to warn off other cats. Since the borders of one's kingdom tend to be the most likely places to encounter greedy or hostile competitors, it's hard to relax and sit down to a hearty meal.

Toys

Perhaps the best argument for providing baubles for your cat is that he will happily use yours if there's nothing more satisfying available. Complexity or novelty is, fortunately, not an issue; in fact, the simpler the toy, the more enjoyment your cat will probably derive from it. A toy can be as unpretentious as a crinkled piece of paper, though your cat may tend to tire of it rather quickly, and ask for another — since his attention is drawn by the crinkling sound itself. Other homespun entertainments include rolled-up aluminum foil, bottle caps, paper grocery bags, and — of course — cardboard boxes.

Plastic or rubber balls can provide hours of amusement, as can furry little mice, or cloth ones stuffed with catnip. For the sake of variety, something dangling on a string or a wire, either attached to a doorknob or extending from a closed dresser drawer, offers an opportunity for a little leaping and tugging.

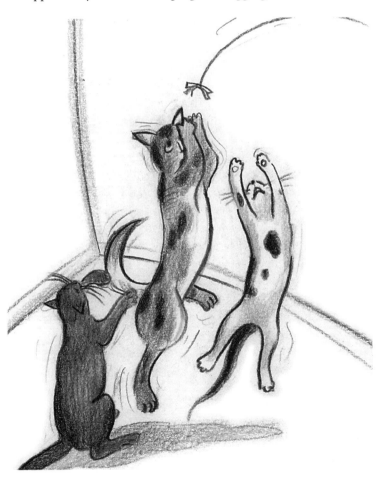

Don't be alarmed if your cat loses interest in a toy after a day or two. He needs time to forget and rediscover it; sometimes his interest can be rekindled more quickly if you participate by throwing or dangling it, or making it crawl across the floor while you make little mousie sounds. Toys also seem to magically disappear under beds, behind laundry baskets, and other locations inaccessible to clever paws. Regular cleaning can help to alleviate this problem, though as a general note, whatever toys you provide for your cat should not be so small that they are quickly lost or easily digested.

Carriers

You'll need something to transport your cat from wherever you acquire her to your home, and occasionally from home to the veterinarian. The cardboard carriers most pet stores and shelters provide are at best only temporary vehicles. A reasonably clever cat can manage to get free with very little trouble. Moreover, since travel can sometimes make a cat nervous, accidents of an excretory or orally projectile nature may occur, irrevocably soiling the box and making the cardboard soggy.

The most common type of carrier is made of hard plastic, with either a wire lid or wire front gate than can be latched in such a way that even an Einstein among cats can't figure out how to open it. Though zippered, soft nylon carriers have enjoyed some popularity, many cats do not feel adequately supported when riding in them. Moreover, many airlines adhere to specific policies regarding acceptable carriers. Should you consider traveling with your cat, you must contact the airline to find out its requirements. Otherwise, you and your cat will end up standing at the window, waving dejectedly at the departing plane.

Grooming Implements

Short-haired cats do not require grooming to the same degree as longhairs. Still, an occasional run-through with a wire or rubber brush can be a pleasant bonding experience for both cat and owner. A wire brush and a comb are essential tools for daily grooming of a long-haired cat.

In addition, you should keep a nail clipper on hand for monthly or bimonthly pedicures. You can purchase a special set of feline clippers or use a toenail clipper. Regular pedicures, though not as appealing a procedure as brushing and combing, will help prevent hangnails and occasional damage to furnishings, ankles and other unprotected areas of the human body. Be sure to offer your cat a treat afterward, to make up for any loss in dignity he suffers in the process.

While certain implements are available for cleaning tartar buildup, it is safe to say that brushing a cat's teeth is not for the fainthearted. Even a complacent Ragdoll is likely to respond adversely to having his mouth thrust open for the purpose of inserting a foreign object. Unless you are blessed with an unusually forgiving animal, it is best to leave oral care to the veterinarian.

HAZARDS OF OCCUPANCY

Cats don't read. Nor do they listen to public service announcements, heed the advice of grandmothers, or find explanations of right and wrong even remotely interesting. They do look before they leap, though in most cases the point of looking is to discover any object that might interfere with a comfortable landing; their sense of distance, or depth perception, is open to debate. They also learn from their mistakes. However, if the mistake happens to be a fatal one, whether they have learned their lesson or not is rather a moot point.

It follows that responsibility for your cat's safety rests squarely on your shoulders. Since what may present a danger to your cat does not necessarily coincide with what may be considered a hazard to your own life, securing your environment for feline occupation can take a bit of foresight. It's reasonable to assume that any object or situation that can harm an active, curious two-year-old may pose a threat to your cat.

Open windows, toxic chemicals, medicines, and anything even remotely connected with heat head the list of obvious perils. Less readily apparent threats include open drawers, holes in the wall or floor, washers and dryers, and yards. Both types of hazards, as well as related precautions, will be discussed in the following sections.

Windows

Movement awakens the feline hunting instinct. It doesn't matter to your cat whether the movement is generated by a flying bird or insect, a squirrel on a nearby tree, or a shiny red car twenty stories below. Once the impulse has arisen, he must give chase. Moreover, cats tend to be inspired by any opportunity to expand their territory. They may be timid at first, but as they become accustomed to the smells and sounds of foreign soil, their courage mounts.

Openings of any sort into realms beyond their customary domain thus present an obvious temptation to even the most sedentary feline. If Pandora happens to live in a high-rise, or even a moderately tall building, a fall from an open window can be fatal — or at the very least, quite damaging. Yet a window leading straight into the front yard may also prove a direct route to death and disease (see "The Not-So-Great Outdoors" on page 114).

The only way to prevent tragedy and still enjoy fresh air is to employ secure screens across your windows. The best kind are those that snap into the window frame itself, usually interchangeable with storm windows. Most apartment buildings, however, do not supply these, and even certain homes are fitted with windows that tilt, rather than slide up or down.

In such cases you will have to erect some sort of screen yourself, either by stretching some sort of durable mesh across the window sash or a frame, or purchasing a prefabricated screen. If you opt for the prefabricated variety, or decide to build your own frame, make sure that it is large enough to encompass the entire width of the open window; an inch of space left open at the very top is acceptable, but don't tempt fate. It is best to secure the screen completely inside the window, rather than between the edge of window and the sill or sash. Otherwise, a rambunctious or persistent cat may push it loose, and find himself taking a magic carpet ride down to the pavement below.

Doors and Other Openings

More or less the same principle holds for any other type of access to the outside world. Since you're fairly likely to use the front or back door several times a day, the best you can do to prevent a daring break for the wild is to look around your feet every time you go out or come in. If Puss is too close for comfort, you can try gently prodding her away with your foot and beat a hasty exit; in some cases, you may have to pick her up and move her bodily to another room. Similarly, any time a repairman or some other visitor spends time in your home, you need to alert them to the presence of a cat. If you're not going to be around for the duration of Uncle Arthur's visit, you should probably exercise caution and put your cat in a closed room, along with his litter box, food bowls, and a couple of toys.

Less obvious means of escape should be considered, as well. Though rare, it is not entirely unheard of for a cat to make a mad dash up the fireplace on occasions of extreme terror. Unless the flue is tiled, bricked surfaces can offer a claw-hold for a determined cat. Fortunately, easy access can be prevented by placing a sturdy, decorative screen in front of the fireplace. Mail slots, meanwhile, usually present a danger only to small cats and kittens; perhaps the best solution involves covering the slot with some sort of metal basket, which will still allow mail to be dropped through, while preventing your cat from exercising his investigatory skills. Finally, French doors that may be opened by a swift pounce on the handles should be kept locked, or else the handles should be tightly secured with a wedge or a stick.

Hot Stuff

Even half an hour after use, the burners on your stove can sear a cat's paws beyond recognition. Likewise, open frying pans or pots in which food is boiling can cause serious damage to paws, coat, eyes, and ears. If you subscribe to the theory that a watched pot never boils, or if you have finished cooking and are ready to sit down to a toothsome meal, it's a good idea to cover all pots and pans, or fill them with cold water if they're empty. At the same time, any burners you've used should be covered over, either with a pot of cool water or a heavy lid.

Similarly, when you've finished pressing your clothes, unplug the iron and set it somewhere your cat does not frequent. Candles, oil lamps, or alcohol lamps should be extinguished if you intend to leave the room for more than a moment. Cats are drawn by the movement and brightness of flames, and can either singe their whiskers or, even more tragic, knock over whatever's burning and cause a fire. For the same reason, if you smoke, never leave a lit cigarette burning in the ashtray. While most cats sensibly abhor the smell, the lazy drift of rising cigarette smoke may override their common sense and compel them to investigate. Even after extinguishing your cigarette, it's still a good idea to empty the ashtray immediately, or remove it to a secure, out-of-the-way place.

Toxins

An open cupboard is an invitation to disaster. Common household cleaning agents, such as ammonia, Lysol, bleach, or grease-cutting sprays, may not necessarily attract your cat, but the open kitchen cupboard or storage cabinet will. In the course of his exploration, your cat may accidentally tip over a bottle. If it isn't tightly closed, the contents may spill and get on his fur or his paws; and in his haste to remove the offending substance from himself, he will ingest large quantities of poison.

Sadly, most poison-control centers have little or no experience with cases of feline poisoning, and before you can rush your cat to the veterinarian or nearest animal hospital, he will most probably suffer an extremely painful death. In addition to attaching a childproof latch to any cupboard or cabinet containing harmful substances, you can safeguard your pet's health by making sure that open containers of cleaning fluid or powder are never left unattended on the floor or counter. Medicinal substances — including pills, syrups, rubbing alcohol, and hydrogen peroxide — should be stored far out of reach, preferably in a securely latched cabinet. Automotive solutions, such as antifreeze, are also extremely toxic. A more complete list of toxic substances can be found in Appendix C.

Plants
Plant-chewing can have a more disastrous effect than leading visitors to question your home gardening skills. Many plants are poisonous — to humans, as well as cats. Among the most common hazards are dieffenbachia, ivy, philodendron, and poinsettia; consult Appendix C for a more complete list. While most cats are discriminating enough to avoid toxic greenery, it's wise to keep handsome specimens out of reach.

Many explanations have been offered for feline attraction to greenery. According to some, cats eat grass or plant leaves in order to induce vomiting, which in turn divests them of particularly troublesome hair balls that cannot be passed by any other means. Others hold that plant material adds roughage or vital nutrients to the diet. Kittens, of course, will chew on anything. Though it may not be perceived as an especially amicable greeting, it's their way of getting to know their world. If your cat persists in gnawing the daisies, he may be trying to compensate for a dietary deficiency. You may try switching to a cat food richer in folic acid, or you might plant a pot of special cat grass, seed for which is available at most pet stores. His own pot of grass should keep Junior out of the marigolds.

Floors, Drawers, and Inside Doors
Be it ever so forbidding, any type of crack or hole promises a world of enchantment to a cat. If she can slide through a hole in the floorboards or a chink in the wall, Miss Kitty cannot help but investigate. In truth, her predilection to explore has less to do with eager curiosity than with an instinctual need to safeguard her territory: A gap represents a potential weakness in her environmental defenses, through which another cat may enter and attack. Logic plays almost no role in this process (as anyone who has suffered in

the grip of instinct can tell you). Despite the unlikelihood of any feline threat, a cat will explore a large vase, a plastic bag, an open refrigerator, a covered radiator, and the terrifying space between the dishwasher and the kitchen cabinets.

Each type of opening represents a specific safety hazard. A cat may easily become wedged inside a radiator or trapped inside a wall or under the floor, and either lacerate or strangle herself in an attempt to escape. She can become tangled inside a plastic bag or closed inside a drawer, and suffocate. She may claim the inside of an open dishwasher, and drown when you bump the door closed and start the machine. Comic misrepresentations notwithstanding, she will not emerge from a dryer cycle all puffed and warm; she will be brutally bludgeoned and burned.

In order to prevent mishaps, always check before closing drawers, cupboard or closet doors, and the door of any type of appliance (including microwaves, freezers, and refrigerators). Before operating a machine, such as a dishwasher, washer, or dryer, make sure your cat is not sleeping inside. Cover empty vases and cracks in the wall or under the furniture, and store plastic bags out of reach.

Cords and Strings

The feline intellect seems to be based on a process of association. You, for example, are associated with food, warmth, other basic comforts, and reprimands. Therefore, you fall under the category of "Mother" (or "God," depending on your cat's capacity for abstraction). In the same vein, anything long and sinuous falls under the generalized heading of "Tail." The only surefire way to determine whether a Tail is connected to something delightful to eat is to chew on it a while.

The results of investigating an electrical cord in this manner can be extremely unpleasant, if not fatal. If you catch your cat attempting to conduct an inquiry of this sort, reprimand him immediately (see Chapter Six for the most appropriate methods of discouraging behavior) and remove him from the area.

Between your reprimands and the rather disagreeable taste of rubberized coating, your cat will likely forgo further exploration. If he persists, you may have to consider wrapping the cords in electrical tape or enclosing them in some sort of tube.

Loose bits of thread, meanwhile — along with ribbons, rubber bands, and strings of any sort — represent another type of hazard. They tend to wriggle around when examined, provoking a determined and thorough investigation. Ultimately, they may be swallowed. Smaller lengths are often simply passed. While cleaning the litter box, for instance, you may discover bits of solid waste connected by a piece of tinsel. Unfortunately, long or thick pieces of string or ribbon are not so easily handled by the feline digestive process. Your cat may very well choke if the string gets caught on his tongue or in his throat. The foreign matter may also become lodged in his stomach or intestines, and prevent him from digesting food or eliminating waste. If you notice your cat choking, gagging, or coughing persistently, seek medical attention immediately. Other symptoms to look for are persistent vomiting, difficulty passing solid waste, or loss of appetite.

If you enjoy watching your cat play with a string or ribbon, make sure you put it away before leaving the room; or else tie it to a chair or doorknob, so he can't swallow it. Tinsel — whether employed on holiday occasions or casually draped around the house for a year-round festive effect — should be kept high on Christmas tree branches or other festooned objects. The same principle applies, incidentally, to glass holiday ornaments. Cats are drawn to shiny things that can easily shatter, and shards of glass can get stuck in paws or swallowed.

Sharp Things and Little Things
Pins, needles, tacks, and staples should be put in containers or discarded. Cats can easily damage their paws by treading on something sharp, or tear their mouths and throats by chewing on them. Earrings and earring backs are particularly tempting targets, since they are shiny and fun to bat around the floor. Knives

and scissors should be returned to their proper homes after use, as a sharp blade can cause considerable harm to an eye or a paw. Fragments of broken glass or porcelain should be swept up immediately; it's not a bad idea to go over the floor with a damp rag or paper towel, to collect anything the vacuum cleaner may have missed.

The Not-So-Great Outdoors

Some people consider it perfectly acceptable to allow their cats to wander unsupervised outside. After all, a cat is a clever creature, and seems attracted enough by what she sees from the window to want to investigate more closely. To this well-meaning, if misguided, sentiment one can only respond, so is a two-year-old. If you feel sanguine about letting a child with only a rudimentary command of language and relatively little understanding of danger play outside by himself for eight or ten hours — then by all means, let your cat outside. When she ends up under the wheel of a car, you have no one to blame but yourself.

Aside from the threat posed by moving vehicles, other hazards stalk outdoor cats. They can, for example, be attacked by other cats, dogs, or wild animals. Contact with other cats can also communicate deadly viruses, such as feline leukemia, feline AIDS, and rabies. A casual stroll through the grass can invite infestations of fleas and worms, which are difficult to control, and if left untreated may lead to more serious health problems.

Specifically human threats abound, as well. Certain types of hooligans, for example, have been known to practice terrible things upon small, unsuspecting animals. Others, whether provoked or not, may put out poison with the intention of killing the neighborhood cat. Even if poison has not been laid down specifically for cats, yours may accidentally pass through a trap laid for another type of animal, or eat a mouse or bird that has been poisoned. Or she may simply swipe a bit of rancid food from the garbage.

In the end, perhaps the simplest message speaks most clearly: Don't let your cat outside. Ever.

WORLDLY TREASURES

You have probably observed that everyday use of your household goods produces a certain amount of wear and tear. Since you probably paid handsomely or put yourself through some other type of hardship to acquire them, you may feel some concern about maintaining their condition for as long as humanly possible. Your cat, however, has probably never had to work a day in his life, and doesn't comprehend the difficulties involved in repairing or replacing a damaged item. In fact, he hasn't the slightest notion of shared ownership. As far as he's concerned, everything in his territory rightfully belongs to him.

Such innocence is charming up to a point. You may be amused to watch Fifi delicately stepping across the top of your great-grandmother's armoire, but when she knocks the Baccarat off the shelf, or claws the curio table originally owned by Napoleon, the sound you make may very well be something other than laughter. If your worldly goods tend to be of the costly, rare, or vintage variety, you should definitely consider adopting one of the more complacent types of cat. Yet, even if you've furnished your apartment with Mom's old Danish Modern, you may feel justifiably protective about your things. After all, lava lamps don't grow on trees.

Damage caused by even a placid Persian rushing to get to the litter box on time can break your heart, especially if the item in question is irreplaceable or has some sentimental significance. While you may learn to let go of certain attachments, the lesson isn't necessarily pleasant. Fortunately, you can take steps to minimize the likelihood of loss or disfigurement to worldly treasures.

Scratchables

Cats claw furniture, clothing, and other articles for a number of reasons. In the first place, scratching is the means by which cats strip away old, worn-out claw sheaths to expose sharp, new claws — a process not unlike a snake shedding its skin. In fact, from time to time, you may actually discover a dried-up old sheath on the floor or stuck in the side of your Louis Vuitton suitcase. Curiously, cats sharpen only their front claws in this manner. They strip their hind claws with their teeth.

Repetitive scratching also serves to exercise the muscles used to extend and retract claws. This keeps them in shape for hunting, attacking, and defense. It's an instinctive mechanism, which can no more be inhibited than breathing.

Finally, clawing is a subtle form of marking territory. Scent glands on the underside of a cat's front paws release chemical secretions when pressed vigorously against cloth, leather, wood, or just about any other type of surface. In this way, cats leave their distinctive odor on territorial possessions, which is one of the clearest means of orienting themselves to their environment: If they recognize their scent on enough objects, they know they're home.

Natural as these functions are, they can nevertheless reduce furniture and other household goods to a sad state of disrepair if you don't supply an alternative outlet. Perhaps the simplest solution is to purchase or build a scratching post. Many commercial varieties are sprayed with catnip oil as an enticement to your cat.

Not all cats respond to scratching posts with equal enthusiasm. You may have to try several different kinds until you find one that meets with your cat's approval; you may also try draping an old article of clothing across the post, since cats are naturally drawn to add their scent to anything that holds yours. Alternatively, you may try tacking a piece of carpeting to a wall, a closet door, or the side of a nightstand or similar piece of furniture. In addition, many pet stores and pet departments offer scratching boards, consisting of a short plank wound with sisal, a strong fibrous type of rope, or nylon cord. Scratching boards can be hung from a doorknob or handle, and are easy to pack for traveling.

Methods of redirecting the focus of an established scratching habit are discussed more fully in Chapter Six. Please note, however, that declawing is not an option. It may have been a popular

disciplinary technique in the 1950s and '60s, but so were a lot of other unspeakable acts. Declawing is popularly misunderstood as a simple removal of the claws; the actual process involves severing the first joint of each finger. It is painful, and may irrevocably alter your cat's personality. Moreover, on the off chance that your cat escapes or wanders outdoors, she will have no means to defend herself against other cats, evil-minded teenagers, or other types of predators.

Breakables and Misplaceables

The principle governing the relationship between cats and objects is Aristotelian in its simplicity: Anything that might bend or break might bend or break. In the course of his daily roaming, even a trustworthy cat may accidentally brush up against your ormolu clock and send it crashing from the mantle to the floor. More mischievous felines may be actively drawn to an especially handsome bud vase, picture frame, or dried flower arrangement.

If he damages an item in the course of exploring it, he can't be held responsible; he's simply expressing his nature. If you don't want to come home to a dining room table strewn with dried leaves or a floor littered with shards of broken glass, make sure all delicate items are securely weighted or attached to their resting place. You might also consider putting them where your cat cannot possibly climb; even so, it's still a good idea to fasten them securely, wherever they eventually settle.

Small items, meanwhile, such as watches, jewelry, pens, paper clips, and coins, should be put away when not actively being used. Desk supplies should go in drawers; jewelry needs a securely fastened box; coins can be gathered in a stoppered or lidded jar. Likewise, items such as answering machines and computer keyboards should be kept out of the cat's path. Otherwise, in the course of his travels, Rex might step on the button that erases all your messages or exits your word-processing program without saving the document you've been slaving over.

SUMMARY

If the foregoing may seem unusually intense or complicated, you're right. Assuming responsibility for a life is no light matter. The good news is, once you've taken reasonable precautions, you won't have to repeat the process (unless, of course, you move). Though your cat's personality will change somewhat as she grows older, the shift is usually in the direction of increased mellowness. Unless she becomes chronically ill or suffers bodily damage, you won't have to worry about fresh threats looming on the horizon. She will never ask for the car keys, or risk expulsion from high school. Unless you're foolish enough to let her outside, she will never go on a date.

Perhaps one of the deepest motivations behind adopting a pet is a nostalgia for the pleasures of childhood. When watching a child at play or at rest, it's not uncommon to wish he'll never grow up, never lose the wonderful innocence and exuberance of youth. To a large extent, cats fulfill such fantasies. They may leap from the dinner table, but they will never fall from grace. To care for one is both a blessing and a most sacred obligation.

CHAPTER 5

The Arrival

At last, the day has come. The screens are up, delicate items have been rearranged, the litter box is filled and ready, the scratching post stands at attention. It's a nice idea to have a bowl of water out, though food probably won't be necessary right away. Your cat will probably be somewhat nervous about traveling with a virtual stranger. Once he or she arrives at your home, there'll be too much sniffing around to do — not to mention a bit of initial rubbing against furniture, ankles, and so on — before relaxing in front of a nice, smelly bowl of cat food.

Attention to a few details can make the transition from your cat's former residence to your home a little more comfortable. Perhaps the most important point to remember is that, while your cat's arrival may be an exciting, joyous moment in your life, the cat will probably see himself as a kind of refugee, torn from familiar surroundings and thrust, uncertainly, on foreign soil. Try to imagine your own response to being shoved in a box, and blindly conveyed at high speed to an utterly strange place where no one speaks your language and you can't make sense of theirs. It's a fairly unsettling picture. From a feline point of view, adoption is on a par with alien abduction.

THE JOURNEY HOME

If you're acquiring a cat from a home, find out in advance if his owner already has a carrier. The trip will prove a lot less disorienting if Pumpkin can travel inside something that smells familiar. A cat's sense of smell, extraordinarily acute under normal circumstances, becomes especially keen in moments of stress. The scent of something he knows will help relax him. If the previous owner can't supply you with a carrier, or if you're acquiring your cat from a store or a shelter, a toy or a piece of his old bedding will serve just as nicely. In any case, the bottom of the carrier should be lined with newspaper or a towel, in case the cat soils himself.

If you're driving home with your new companion, consider taking someone along to hold the carrier and talk to the cat during the trip home. Most cats respond well to the soothing sound of a human voice and the warmth and smell of a human body. Car windows should be closed to minimize traffic noises; you should probably also refrain from playing the radio or tape deck, as sudden changes in decibel level can cause the cat to panic. Under no circumstances should you allow a cat or kitten to roam freely through the vehicle on your first car trip together. Cats are notoriously unpredictable when nervous, and your little friend may suddenly decide to make a dash for your head (or the brake pedal) at a most inopportune moment.

If you are traveling by public transportation, hold the carrier close to your body and talk softly to the cat. People sitting near you may glance at you rather strangely until they realize you're reassuring a small, terrified animal, and not simply holding a conversation with your overcoat. It's probably not a good idea to push your fingers inside the carrier or place your face too close to the grate. Under duress, many cats produce an excess of adrenaline that triggers a state commonly referred to as the fight-or-flight response — similar in form and function to the human reaction to a disconnect notice from the telephone company. Unable to flee, your cat may lash out with his claws.

If you are walking home with your new friend, holding the carrier close to your body may prove unduly taxing. You might consider stopping every few minutes and supporting the carrier with both hands. This will mitigate the unpleasant effects of swinging somewhat loosely back and forth in rhythm with your stride. As you pause, you may wish to lift the carrier near your face, and say something nice.

INTRODUCING THE HOUSEHOLD

Once you've arrived home, resist the impulse to tear open the carrier door and pull your cat out. Intimacy, even when purchased, can't be rushed. Patience is key to a satisfying beginning of any new relationship. If you've acquired your cat from a home, he's been separated from friends and family. Even if you've rescued a cat from the street or from a shelter, he'll need time to find and display his gratitude.

One Room at a Time

When you arrive home, place your cat's carrier in the room where his litter box is located and close the door behind you. It's best to be alone with him at this stage; too many people in one room will make him anxious. However, if you have children, and they're brokenhearted at the prospect of being left out of the introduction, advise them to be as quiet as possible, and to let the cat come to them.

Now, open the carrier door and let the cat emerge on his own. This will probably happen slowly. Until he has become familiar with his new lair, he will consider it unfriendly. Point out his litter box, either by scratching inside it or gently shaking it. If necessary, place him very gently inside it. He may or may not begin scratching the litter to mark it; if you've adopted a kitten, try working his wee paws in the litter for a few seconds until he gets the point.

As your cat begins to investigate the room, talk to him softly. Don't make any sudden moves, though you may hold out your hand for an exploratory sniff. If he remains close to you, try stroking him behind his ears or under his chin; he may even let you run your hand across his back. At this point, your cat may or may not be quite ready to be held.

The Rest of the House

Once the cat appears to have adjusted to her new surroundings, you can open the door and allow her to roam a little farther. If possible, confine this exploration to one room at a time, so as not to overburden her senses. At this point, other human members of the household may be introduced, preferably one at a time, since your pet will have to catalogue the scent of everyone he or she meets. Ask each person to speak softly and call the cat by name, perhaps extending a hand for him or her to sniff.

Children should be shown how to hold a cat. It is never appropriate to lift a cat up by the scruff of its neck. Only its natural mother or a feline surrogate can manage that trick without inflicting pain. The proper way to lift and hold a cat is by sliding one hand around its chest, under the front paws, and supporting its back legs with the other hand; its back should rest comfortably in the crook of the arm that holds the back paws. After being lifted calmly, many cats enjoy being cradled in the arms like a baby. Some, however, are absolutely appalled by such treatment. A lot depends on mood — yours and your cat's. If you're both peaceful and relaxed, the experience can be very moving.

Younger children, especially, need to be warned against hanging on too tightly if the cat doesn't want to be held. Explain to them that cats have sharp claws and teeth, and will use them to get away. Also, make sure children understand that cats are not toys, and as a rule do not enjoy being bathed, dressed in doll clothes, or dragged about on a leash. You might show them how to attract the cat's attention with a toy or a piece of string. This type of play will likely keep most children occupied until the novelty of ownership wears thin, and they start yearning for whatever novelty the neighbor's kids have just acquired.

If You're Adopting a Kitten

Kittens bond very tightly with their mothers and siblings, and will often be sad and frightened upon finding themselves alone for the first time in their lives. Do your best to soothe a little one by answering his woeful cries, stroking him, and letting him crawl up into your lap, your shoulder, or inside the crook of your arm. Ideally, a kitten's first few days in a new home should be quiet and calm. While inherited traits are a major factor in the development of temperament, environment plays an equally significant role. Consistently loud noises or sudden movements can send a little cat scrambling terrified toward the nearest dark, secure place — and a lifetime habit of anxiety. A kitten treated with respect and gentleness will usually grow into a sociable, affectionate cat.

Frequent play periods, meanwhile, can facilitate the socialization process. Plan on devoting three or four ten-minute periods a day to simple games like "Dangle the Key Chain" and "Bat the Ball till You're Exhausted," then wind down with a calm round of "Nuzzle Baby's Belly." Not only will your kitten begin to look on you as a special friend, but you'll probably feel a little lightening of your spiritual load.

Kittens need a good deal of supervision and reassurance. During his first couple of weeks in your home, he may cry for attention with alarming frequency. In time he'll outgrow his utter dependence on you. More important, kittens are apt to find themselves in very strange predicaments. They may, for instance, wriggle and leap to the top of a bookcase without the slightest notion how to get down. Until he's stronger and more coordinated, you'll have to help him out of any fix he can't manage on his own. Also, take care to look around the floor before closing doors. A slammed door can easily crush a kitten rushing to follow you.

If You're Adopting an Older Cat

In general, older cats require somewhat less supervision, and can adapt more readily to a new home. Still, older cats may show signs of emotional distress. A new environment, devoid of familiar shapes and smells, can be terribly disorienting. Some older cats may have been so attached to their former owners that grief and homesickness actually overwhelm them. Others may have had bad experiences with people or animals; certain noises or a lot of traffic in the house may terrify them. Some may have been so emotionally shattered they distrust everyone and everything on principle.

Understanding and patience are the best remedies. It's a good idea to provide a safe haven the cat can run to when she feels threatened. Leave out food for her on a regular basis, even if she doesn't come running when she hears the can opener. When she's around, talk to her in a soothing tone, calling her by name; and allow her to come to you when she's ready. Don't force anything. Cats possess an extraordinarily delicate sense of trust, and a clumsy move on your part too early on in your acquaintance can easily shatter it.

If You Already Have a Cat (or Two)

If you have another cat, you can be sure he or she will look on the newcomer as an invader, and will almost certainly attempt to defend its territory. In the wild, an intruder would either retreat or fight for possession of the territory; in a domestic situation, the first scenario is impossible, while the second is undesirable. As a general rule, allow the new arrival to meet other household cats only after it has explored most of the other rooms and met most of the other humans. Don't leave an established cat and a newcomer alone together for the first few days; if you must go out, keep them in separate rooms. Also, be sure each cat has its own food dish, so there is no competition at mealtimes. You may even have to use separate litter boxes until the cats have established friendly relations.

In many respects, introducing a kitten to an older cat is far easier than introducing two mature cats to one another. Through a combination of naked need, adoration, and natural ebullience, a kitten can usually win over even the most hardhearted or possessive cat. The process usually takes about a week. Initially, the older cat will growl, hiss, and give the upstart what-for with his paws and teeth. Gradually, his resistance will diminish, as the kitten accepts a subordinate position in the social hierarchy. Once you catch the two cats touching noses, you will know that an important bridge has been crossed.

During the period of adjustment, it is extremely important to shower affection on the older cat. He won't demand it; in fact, he may behave atrociously — turning on you when you approach, shredding toilet paper, or leaving unwelcome packages on your pillow. Nevertheless, you must persist in giving him special attention. If he lets you pick him up, hold him in your lap more often than you usually do. Scratch him behind the ears, tell him how handsome, wise, and strong he is: He won't believe a word of it, but he'll appreciate the effort. Probably the clearest message is an edible one, though. Give him treats — lots of them — and feed him a little extra at mealtimes. A full belly frequently engenders a mellow attitude.

Introducing an older cat into a household ruled by another cat can be tricky, since you can't rely on kittenish behavior to charm the head of the household. The key, really, is to make sure there is adequate space in your home for each cat to claim some territory of its own. As when introducing a kitten into the household, you must shower attention on the established cat, and never leave the animals together unsupervised until you are certain they have signed a peace treaty that allows at least for peaceful coexistence (occasional wrestling matches aside). If they persist in attacking one another after a couple of months, or if you are reduced to feeding them in separate rooms, you may wish to consider finding a new home for the most recent adoptee.

Cats and Dogs Together

The notion that cats and dogs despise one another on principle is pure fantasy. While some interspecies discord may be observed, the main impediment to harmonious relations is one of language. Broadly speaking, signs common to the languages of both species express entirely opposite meanings. A dog wagging its tail usually intends to suggest friendliness, whereas cats wag their tails when they're confused or annoyed. Cats translate quick movements as aggression, while dogs see leaping or jumping as an invitation to play. And so on.

Kittens and puppies raised together usually have little problem learning each other's language. Their natural curiosity tends to overcome any resentment or embarrassment generated by unintended insults. A kitten will also generally respond well to an older dog, provided the older dog does not frighten or injure him by playing too roughly. An older cat brought into a home occupied by a dog may never become overtly friendly; though as long as she can carve out a few islands of sanctuary for herself around the home, all should be well.

Naturally, all early encounters between cats and dogs of any age should be strictly supervised. It's also a good idea to consult a veterinarian or a breeder to find out if your specific breed of dog is temperamentally tolerant of cats. For optimum harmony, consider adopting a cat whose breed tends to get along with dogs.

Other Types of Pets

In general, cats and kittens form fast friendships with animals roughly their own size. They can, for example, exist quite peaceably with rabbits and large guinea pigs. Smaller animals, however, will generally be viewed as a potential dinner. Hamsters, mice, and lizards should never be allowed to roam freely around a cat; the results have been known to turn even a brave stomach. Aquariums, meanwhile, should be securely fitted with covers, since neon tetras and zebra danios are apt to be viewed as finger food.

While small birds should always be kept securely latched in inaccessible cages, parrots or other large birds may, under close supervision, be allowed loose around a cat. Bear in mind that big birds typically have sharp beaks and won't hesitate to use them if provoked. Should nature suddenly overcome household manners, each side may suffer extremely serious damage.

Bonding

Touch is vital to a cat's physical and emotional well-being. Physical bonding begins immediately after birth, when a mother cat licks and grooms each of her kittens, stimulating its circulation and digestive tract. Gentle caressing and licking, together with the warmth of its mother's body, inspire feelings of security and closeness in the newborn. Kittens deprived of this early stage of physical bonding often grow up neurotic, skittish, and terrified of being handled; in some cases illness develops or the kitten may refuse to eat, and thus weakened, may even die.

When you hold your cat, and stroke her gently behind the ears or under the chin, you build positive, warm feelings between you and her. In feline terms, you are creating the deepest and most lasting kind of bond imaginable: You have, in effect, become her mother — weirdly hairless, perhaps, but warm, soothing, and wholesome. The contented purr of a cat that has learned to trust you can be one of the sweetest sounds on earth. And though her tongue is like wet sandpaper, when you feel its rough magic on your arm or on your face, it's the highest compliment of all. As far as your cat is concerned, you've now risen to the rank of equal.

First Visit to the Vet

It is absolutely essential to have your new pet thoroughly examined by a veterinarian within a week of adopting her. Trust no one's word otherwise in this regard. Unless you have personally accompanied the previous owner to the vet, you can't be certain of your cat's health status. Ask friends or neighbors to recommend a veterinarian with whom they feel comfortable; local breeders may likewise provide reliable recommendations. You might also check with your local humane society or shelter for the names of doctors associated with the organization.

In making your choice, consider the following factors:

- Accreditation by a state or national veterinary association
- Convenient location
- Reasonable hours
- Sanitary conditions of the office or clinic
- 24-hour emergency service coverage
- Membership in organizations such as the American Animal Hospital Association, Feline Practitioners Association, American Association of Veterinary Cardiology, or the Animal Behavior Association — while not essential — suggests that a veterinarian is actively interested in new developments in medical treatments

Don't be shy of asking questions. It's important to establish a good rapport with your veterinarian, since your cat's health will rest in his hands for many years to come.

During the initial visit, the veterinarian will check your cat's body temperature, teeth, and eyes, as well as examine his coat for fleas and his ears for mites. When you make the appointment, let

the receptionist know that this is your cat's first visit, and ask whether a stool sample will be necessary. A sample is often required to determine the presence of internal parasites. If you have any records of your cat's prior medical history, bring them along so the vet can decide whether or not vaccinations or boosters are necessary (a discussion of vaccinations can be found in Chapter Six).

Especially if your cat is unused to, or not overtly fond of, traveling, it's a good idea to avoid feeding him for a few hours before the trip. Line the carrier with newspaper, and include a favorite toy or piece of clothing that carries the cat's scent. Many cats will not willingly enter a carrier. It is best to perform this sometimes grueling task quickly, calmly, efficiently; though you may be tempted to scream, speak quietly and lovingly to your cat. In addition, you might wish to wear clothing that protects your arms and legs. Under no circumstances should you attempt to pet or rub your face against an angry, outraged cat.

Keep talking to him all the way to the vet's office. Once you're seated in the waiting room, hold the carrier close to your body so other animals will not be tempted to investigate. If no other patients are around, and if you're absolutely sure you can control any sudden impulses from your cat to flee, scratch, or bite, you may take him out of his carrier and hold him in your lap.

Some cats submit quite passively to the prodding and poking they undergo in the course of a routine examination. Others become understandably indignant when introduced to a rectal thermometer. On the whole, very few cats suffer injections in humble silence. Once the ordeal is over, praise your cat lavishly for behaving so admirably — even if he hasn't comported himself especially well. When you return home, give him something very nice to eat, and assure him that you can both look forward now to a long and happy life together.

THE FIRST MONTH

In an ideal world, kittens are put up for adoption only after they are ten or twelve weeks old. By this time, they've perfected certain skills, such as leaping, scratching, pouncing, and grooming, and have gained a thorough understanding of the difference between the litter box and the carpet. The socialization process has been completed, and whatever good habits she has learned from her mother and the people around her are imprinted for life.

Unfortunately, the same can be said for any bad habits she may have acquired along the way. If the kitten hasn't enjoyed much human contact during the first seven or eight weeks of her life — or worse, has suffered abuse, neglect, or abandonment — she is apt to remain somewhat shy around people for the rest of her life. Stress or mistreatment of any sort leaves a powerful imprint on a kitten's psyche (just as it does with children). Kind, gentle treatment may mitigate the effects somewhat, but may never entirely overcome deep psychological scars.

Similarly, if a kitten has been allowed to develop certain undesirable habits, such as begging at mealtimes, clawing the sofa, or soiling the rug behind the TV set, you will need to use a firm hand to redirect her behavior. In the case of older cats, unpleasant habits may have become so deeply entrenched, they may never be entirely broken. Patience and persistence are essential in overcoming the effects of inadequate socialization. Above all, you must remember that when she does something unacceptable, she is not a bad cat: She's a good cat who has suffered neglect or abuse on a scale you can never begin to imagine. Even more than a properly socialized cat, she needs your love and acceptance.

The Litter Box
Most cats will already be housebroken by the time you adopt them. There are exceptions, of course, particularly among cats born outside a home environment. As described earlier in the chapter, one of the first orders of business when you bring a cat into your home is to introduce him to the litter box. Many cats will recognize its function right away, and remember its location without any reinforcement.

Occasionally, though, you may have to help jog his memory. Kittens typically need a bit more reinforcement than older cats; in either case, you need to keep an eye out for signs of uncertainty. When a cat feels the call of nature and is not sure where to answer it, he will usually meow, look around, scratch the floor, and squat with his tail upraised. It is best to catch him before he squats, though in most cases he will refrain from voiding anything as soon as you touch him. Lift him gently, quickly carry him to the litter box, and set him inside. You may have to stand out of his line of sight while he completes the business at hand. When he does, praise him generously, scratch his ears if he allows (he may feel too embarrassed), and give him a treat. Cats, like people, respond most effectively to tangible rewards.

Scratching Posts

As mentioned earlier, scratching is a necessary feline ritual. Even cats who have been viciously declawed by sadistic owners still go through the motions of stretching out their front legs and vigorously kneading a rough surface. When introduced to a new environment, your cat will not necessarily know where to perform this essential exercise, so it's up to you to show him.

You can speed the process a bit by keeping the scratching post or other device in a readily accessible location. In the course of his initial exploration of your home, he will probably approach the post and sniff it; then again, he may simply pass by warily or disdainfully. In any event, as he approaches it, you can gently lift his paws to the post and manipulate them while cooing a few approving remarks. However, if he shies from your touch on his first day home, you ought not to attempt this, since he will inevitably associate the scratching post with an invasion of his personal space.

Whether or not you are able to introduce him to the scratching post right away, your cat will probably make some initial attempts to scratch various pieces of furniture. He's not only marking his territory, but also testing the waters of what is acceptable and what is not. During the first month of your life together, it's crucial that you carry him to the scratching post every time you catch him clawing the rug or the furniture; otherwise, he'll assume you don't care. If you simply resort to screeching at him, throwing something, or other violent reprisals, he will only become sneaky.

The best approach is to say "No," firmly but quietly, and carry him to the scratching post. You may have to repeat the process of moving his paws on the post. Afterwards, praise him and give him a treat. As we will discuss later on in Chapter Six, effective training utterly depends on association of good behavior with a positive response from you.

Mealtimes

Cats are creatures of habit. They like to be fed at regular times, though breakfast seems to be the most vigorously enforced meal. Once they've come to associate the alarm clock with a dish full of food, cats will anticipate the barely audible click just before the buzzer sounds. Woe betide the would-be dozer, or any owner who has the chance to occasionally sleep in. Your cat will try a number of strategies to rouse you from the bed, most of them amusing. Some cats can be satisfied with cuddling awhile, but more persistent animals will not be fooled by alternative expressions of affection. If you really want to sleep in, the only thing to do is get up, feed the cat, and beat a hasty retreat to the bedroom.

Ideally, you should establish a morning and an evening feeding. If you work away from home, this is a fairly simple routine: Your cat will expect to be fed once when you rise, and again when you return home. If you feed him fairly quickly after you come home, chances are he will leave you in peace while you prepare your own dinner. Beware offering additional snacks while you are preparing your meals: He will come to expect them.

People who work at home need to be exceptionally vigilant. Once a cat has learned that he can manipulate an extra meal or two by standing on your desk or perching, vulturelike, on the laser printer, it will take a firm hand to break a habit you've instilled in him. The same holds for letting your cat enjoy samples from your plate. If you let him lap up the milk at the bottom of your cereal bowl even once, he'll expect it every morning — and probably take umbrage should you change your routine by making pancakes.

Typical serving size depends on the age and activity rate of the cat in question:

- *Kittens between seven and twelve weeks* can easily gobble down between eight and nine ounces of food per day, divided into roughly five servings.

- *Adolescents between the ages of three and seven months* can consume up to twelve and a half ounces of food per day, divided into three servings.

- *Adult cats, from the age of seven months onwards,* will gradually reduce the amount they eat. By the time they're a year old, most cats thrive happily on a mere four and a half ounces of food, divided into two servings. Larger cats, like Manx or Norwegian forest cats, may require more food, while smaller breeds such as Abyssinians can get along on a little less. A Sphynx can polish off a hearty five or six ounces a day without getting fat.

- *Pregnant cats* do not generally require much more food than an average adult, though whatever you serve her should be richer in nutrients, and divided over the course of several meals. Nursing mothers require a good deal more food, up to sixteen ounces per day, divided into several portions.

- *Less active or overweight cats* can usually be served the same amount of food as an average adult, providing it is a "light" brand. As a general rule, though, the diet of an older or overweight cat is best determined by a veterinarian.

Prepared Foods

In the wild, cats usually eat the entire body of their prey. This includes flesh, bones, organs, fur, feathers, and whatever happens to be in the victim's stomach at the time — usually some form of grain or other vegetation. Nature thus supplies them with a balanced diet, high in protein, but also rich in vitamins, minerals, carbohydrates, moisture, and with sufficient fat to keep their coats glossy and to ease the passage of hair balls.

The domestic cat, though expending somewhat less energy in the pursuit of prey, nevertheless requires the same type of balanced diet. Fortunately, many commercially prepared foods supply the right proportions of all the vital nutrients a cat needs. They are typically available in four varieties:

Moist, canned food consists of cooked muscle meats, organ meats, fish, carbohydrates, vitamins, and minerals. Recent studies have shown that taurine is essential for healthy vision, so be sure that whatever brand you serve contains this compound. "Scientifically formulated" brands, available through pet stores and veterinarians, tend to achieve the best nutritional balance; many of these brands are available in specific formulas for kittens, nursing mothers, overweight cats, and less active cats. Among commercial or supermarket brands, the difference in nutritional value is usually negligible; almost any brand will satisfy the needs of a healthy adult cat. Nevertheless, many commercial brands contain nonnutritive fillers, such as gelatin or vegetable products. While not harmful in themselves, such fillers pass directly through your cat's digestive tract. Ounce by ounce, this represents a waste of money that could be spent more wisely. Also, meat and organ meats should be listed ahead of other ingredients, such as meat by-products, to ensure that your cat receives an optimum supply of protein.

Dry foods usually contain a well-balanced mix of proteins, vitamins, and minerals, providing a wholesome diet for most cats. Since dry food typically contains only about ten percent water it's easy to store, lasts for months, and can be left in the bowl at all times — so your cat can help himself to many small meals rather than depend on one or two big meals. Dry foods offer the additional advantage of reducing tartar on your cat's teeth. While some people swear by a diet of dry food alone, the relatively low moisture content means plenty of fresh water must be available at all times. Yet the amount of water a cat drinks does not usually compensate for the moisture obtained from moist food, and various health complications may result. Neutered males subsisting on an exclusively or primarily dry diet frequently suffer urinary tract blockage, which can be fatal if not treated quickly. Therefore, dry food should be given sparingly.

Semimoist foods derive their protein content and fat from a variety of animal and vegetable sources. Typically, the primary source establishes flavor. Semimoist foods contain about thirty to thirty-five percent water and do not inhibit dental tartar. Like dry foods, semimoist varieties tend to emit a far more subtle odor than moist foods. Packaging usually consists of airtight pouches, so they can be stored relatively easily. They can be left in the bowl for about twenty-four hours before going stale. Unfortunately, they also tend to be high in calories and contain quite a lot of preservatives, which cats cannot metabolize as quickly as people.

Gourmet/treat foods do not usually supply a balanced supply of proteins, vitamins, and minerals. Consequently, they should not form the basis of your cat's diet, but should be offered solely as rewards or an occasional holiday meal.

Home-Cooked Meals

A variety of tasty dishes can be made by the enterprising home chef. From time to time, well-meaning individuals have attempted to create a wholesome vegetarian diet for their cats. This is only acceptable if the owner is willing to subsist for the rest of his life on a diet made up exclusively of small bits of newsprint. Cats are carnivores. In order to survive, they must eat meat.

Should you decide to prepare your own food, bear in mind that each meal should consist of meat for protein; saturated and unsaturated fats (polyunsaturated fats, like margarine, do not usually find their way into a carnivore's diet); sugars, starches, and other carbohydrates; cereals, grass, and certain leafy vegetables; organs; and bones or bonemeal. The following foods may be used as a guide:

Meat of just about any variety is the best source of protein for a cat. It should never be served raw; light cooking kills parasites. Cheap, fatty cuts of meat will provide the fat your cat needs.

Fish must be thoroughly boned and cooked. Raw fish can lead to vitamin B1 deficiency. Cod, tuna, and other types of oily fish should be generally avoided, as they have been known to produce vitamin E deficiency, skin problems, and lethargy. Fish organs should never be served.

Eggs provide protein, sulfur, calcium, phosphorous, and a number of other nutrients. They must be served cooked however, though your cat must tell you if he prefers them scrambled, boiled, or over easy.

Liver (either beef or chicken) supplies vitamin A and iron. It should not be offered as the primary ingredient, however, since too much may lead to vitamin A toxicity. Liver should be lightly cooked. Undercooked liver can cause diarrhea; overcooked, it can lead to constipation.

Kidneys are an excellent source of iron and several critical vitamins. Since they also contain a high degree of uric acid, they should be soaked for one or two hours in cold water prior to cooking.

Heart is an exceedingly rich source of protein and high-quality fat.

Milk is not a substitute for water. As a food, it is an excellent source of calcium, phosphorous, and a host of other vitamins and minerals. However, many adult cats are unable to digest milk properly. If your cat develops diarrhea within six or seven hours of drinking milk, he is lactose intolerant. (If he craves milk, you might try an acidophilus-enriched variety.)

Plain yogurt is a handy source of calcium and phosphorous, and is readily digestible by lactose-intolerant felines.

Cheese, while providing calcium, fat, and a moderate amount of protein, can cause irregularity. It is best served sparingly.

Butter provides a rich source of fat, which is necessary to maintain a glossy coat and healthy skin. It is also extraordinarily tempting to even the most discriminating feline palate. Never leave a stick of butter unattended.

Margarine passes right through a cat's digestive system, and ought only to be used as an aid to passing hair balls, or to mitigate the effects of eating too much cheese.

Bones can provide calcium, phosphorous, and other important minerals. Although most cats find beef bones too big to gnaw on, a nice knuckle or tailbone may serve. The bones of smaller animals are easier to chew, but should be lightly boiled to kill parasites. Avoid bird bones, as they might shatter and become lodged in your cat's throat or puncture his stomach wall. As a rule, bonemeal provides a more readily combinable supply of calcium and phosphorous.

Vegetable matter, in small amounts, add taste, texture and carbohydrates to the diet. A tiny bit of cooked potato or rice may be added to round out a meal. Some cats have been known to enjoy corn on the cob and other plain vegetables. To minimize intestinal distress, all vegetables should be thoroughly cooked.

Other cats enjoy cereals such as oatmeal, farina, and cornmeal mush; these should never be served raw, as cats cannot digest the heavy starches. Grits and hominy, meanwhile, should be strictly avoided.

An adult cat's daily ration of home-cooked food will consist of three-and-a-half ounces of meat, a tablespoon of liver or other organ meat, a teaspoon of brewer's yeast (rich in vitamin B complex), and a half teaspoon of bonemeal. In addition, you may add a tablespoon of cooked rice, pasta, or baby cereal, a teaspoon of oil, a tablespoon of cottage cheese, and perhaps a tablespoon or two of strained cooked carrots.

The meat must be cut into bite-sized pieces. Alternatively, you may pass all the ingredients through a meat grinder or food processor. Once you've mixed everything together, make sure it is cool enough to avoid burning your cat's mouth.

Finally, you must be prepared for the possibility that, after all your hard work, your cat may actually prefer canned food. It's not a comment on your cooking skills. You're simply not a cat, so you cannot predict what will appeal to the feline palate and what, ultimately, may be deemed revolting.

CHAPTER 6

The Next Eleven Months

There comes a point in almost any relationship when novelty gives way to familiarity. Broadly speaking, one of two events occurs at this point: Either disillusionment sets in, or an intimacy of a deeper sort begins to take root.

Much depends on the character of the participants. At the first sign of disappointment, some recommence their search for happiness in other quarters. Others, either as a result of prior experience or through plain intuition, understand and appreciate the value of discontent. The pain of imperfection becomes for them a starting point, a means of participating more generously in their own lives and in the world.

Your true mettle as a cat owner will be tested, not by how well you prepare your home or how thoroughly you research your breed, but by how you relate to your cat after the initial excitement of your acquaintance begins to fade. It's not uncommon for owners to come to regard their pets as little more than occasionally interesting ornaments. Most cats willingly accept such treatment in exchange for certain physical and emotional satisfactions; in no way does it constitute abuse or neglect. Yet even the most benign form of inattention exacts a price. There are no boring cats, only owners who pass up the opportunity to explore a wilder, more spontaneous side of themselves.

This chapter examines several levels of participation, some of which are optional, while others cannot be ignored. They include:

- Training
- Travel
- Grooming
- Breeding
- Veterinary care

Medical care, of course, absolutely requires attention. Other issues, such as grooming and breeding, will depend on the type of cat you adopt. Training and travel offer more latitude; and since the concept of choice tends to be more appealing than any notion of necessity, we'll begin by exploring those topics that afford the greatest freedom.

TRAINING

The idea of training cats has met with a certain amount of skepticism over the years. This attitude has evolved, in large part, as a by-product of the relative ease with which dogs learn to heed commands. However, a dog is instinctively attuned to obey the strongest and most intelligent member of his pack. One might say that obedience is the central fact of a dog's life, since his survival, and that of the pack, depends on it. In this light, all canine behavior can be seen as an attempt either to dominate or conform.

Many people mistakenly assume that feline intelligence is organized according to the same principle; when training fails, they compound ignorance with bad judgment and blame the cat. Yet, as Mark Twain once observed, "Of all God's creatures there is only one that cannot be made the slave of the lash. That one is the cat." While a cat will respond to discipline, his motivation is rarely fear. Perhaps for this reason, those of a somewhat puritanical turn of mind tend to distrust cats.

A Few Words About Feline Evolution

Throughout most of the Proterozoic Era, which began some two and a half billion years ago, the consumption of food seems to have been a fairly disorganized affair. With the exception of algae (which remains to this day a fairly hapless animal), every living organism was just as likely to be eaten as to eat. After two billion years of this nonsense, some creatures decided they'd had enough, and began to grow certain hard areas along various portions of their bodies — both to shield themselves from attack as well as to devour their neighbors more efficiently.

Some of these developments proved more ingenious than others, and the creatures who owned the rights to them prospered. As their descendants increased in strength and numbers, they naturally began to compete among themselves, refining and adapting various body parts as the need for self-protection and more sophisticated hunting skills demanded. One of the more satisfying refinements occurred about sixty million years ago, among a race of creatures known as miacids, one of the first classes of truly flesh-eating mammals.

Whereas creatures who follow a more rounded diet use their back teeth to grind vegetable matter into a coarse paste suitable for ingestion, miacids developed extremely sharp molars, called carnassials. Carnassials are designed specifically to slice flesh in a scissorlike action. Further, the powerful miacid jaw moves strictly up and down, allowing none of the lateral movement associated with grinding; this limited range of motion reduces the chance that one's meal might suddenly wriggle out of one's mouth. In addition, two sets of curved fangs prove extremely useful in holding a struggling vole or mouse in place while the carnassials do their work.

Over time, various groups of miacids improved on the basic design in different ways. The modern carnivore family includes a number of distinctive branches, including walruses, seals, bears, dogs, weasels, raccoons, and cats. Yet while many of these animals have adapted to a wider diet, only cats and polar bears remain staunchly carnivorous. Even dogs can subsist on a more variegated diet, and their back teeth include molars as well as carnassials. For sixty million years, while herbivores and omnivores adjusted their diets in accordance with sometimes devastating climatic changes, cats have kept troth with meat.

The approach has its drawbacks, of course. If one is going to depend on one category of food to the exclusion of all others, one had better be darned good at catching it. Accordingly, the entire physiognomy of a cat has evolved around the central importance of hunting and killing live prey. Cats can leap from a standing position up to five times their own height. Using their tails as rudders, they can twist their bodies in free fall and land on four feet to resume a chase at full tilt. The structure of their eyes allows a panoramic view of everything forward of their ears, even in near-dark conditions. Movement stimulates perception; at twenty paces, they can spot a tiny insect crawling about, though they are apt to ignore a hamster paralyzed with fear.

Other senses show similar enhancement. For example, a cat's ears can register a range of sounds more than three times wider than human hearing can detect. His sense of smell is amplified by a structure in his mouth that can detect infinitesimal traces of airborne particles. Known as Jacobson's organ, this tiny opening uses a combination of smell and taste to create precise, multidimensional "odor memories." His whiskers, meanwhile, serve as antennae, measuring not only the dimensions of any gap through which he might hope to squeeze in the course of a hunt, but also subtle vibrations of air bouncing off solid objects. This allows him to move around in the dark without bumping into things, as well as to determine the size and shape of prey he can't necessarily see.

Add to these powers a finely tuned set of reflexes, amazing speed, and a camouflaged coat, and you have a nearly perfect hunting and killing machine. A cat requires no assistance in the hunt, and is rarely — if ever — surprised by an intruder. Since he does not need to live in a pack, the whole issue of obedience or discipline never arises. Only when he is a kitten may his survival depend on the kindness of other cats.

Training Essentials

The key to successful training lies in knowing what your cat wants and what he needs. He wants meat, and in the wild he is fully capable of obtaining it on his own. Domestication, however, renders him permanently kittenish, and he needs you to feed him. In essence, you are your cat's primary source of meat. If it helps to think of yourself as a walking rib roast, then by all means do so. Should you forget this essential relation, however, you may as well chuck the balls, hoops, and spray bottles. Better yet, give them to your cat, because he has already succeeded in training you.

During the first few weeks of life, kittens are entirely dependent on their mother for nourishment. As her brood grows older, she teaches them how to fend for themselves, shaping their inherent leaping, pouncing, and striking skills by encouraging imitation of her own behavior and occasionally resorting to reprimands. Through it all, the connection between mother and food is never entirely forgotten.

Building on this association is a relatively simple matter when you adopt a kitten, since the little one readily transfers his dependency more or less directly onto you. Lay down the rules while he is still impressionable, and he is yours forever. If you wait until bad habits take hold, you are in the same position as someone who adopts an older cat that has learned to live by his own laws. In this case, the greater part of training will consist of establishing and reinforcing limitations until your cat has curtailed unpleasant behavior (at least while you're within earshot).

Successful training rests on a firm foundation of four key principles:

- Trust
- Reward
- Reprimand
- Consistency

All four are needed to produce the desired result. Leave one out, and like a house of cards, your efforts will more than likely collapse.

Trust

Establishing trust necessarily precedes any attempt to influence feline behavior. You can hand out treats until your arm falls off, but if your cat doesn't feel safe, she'll either snatch them and run or wait until you've left the room. At best, the lessons you attempt to teach will be only fitfully remembered.

In order to instill a sense of confidence and reliability, you need to take your cue from a mother cat. She is, first and foremost, a calm, methodical teacher. Never in the annals of feline history has a mother cat resorted to screaming obscenities at the top of her lungs, or thrown her child, however naughty, across the room. Reprimands are administered promptly and without malice: A swat of the paw or a swift shake by the scruff of the neck gets the point across effectively.

Further, a mother cat purrs as she nurses her kittens; and kittens, as they drink her milk, respond by purring. This form of communication, unique to smaller members of the feline species, signals an open, friendly attitude. Curiously enough, it does not always signal contentment. Injured or dying cats also purr, as a means of communicating their need for warmth and solace. People can't purr, of course, but cats seem to understand soothing speech as roughly equivalent. In fact, they are quite generous in accepting this regrettable shortcoming of the human species.

Rewards

Whatever else you may have learned on your mother's knee, the old saw about attracting more bees with honey than with vinegar may be considered gospel. A willing cat responds far more easily to training than a cat who doesn't want to perform. Rewards offered promptly after good behavior will etch a lesson in your cat's brain more deeply than a thousand reproofs.

Two types of reward seem generally acceptable to cats: food and praise. Of the two, food is the preferred choice. In fact, any kind of behavior you would like to encourage must be reinforced with a tasty treat; otherwise, your cat won't see the point of repeating it. Don't think for a minute he'll learn to accept the happy sound of your voice as a substitute for a snack, no matter how strongly you associate the two.

When training your cat to perform some delightful piece of behavior, such as jumping through a hoop or dancing in a circle, give him his reward immediately after completing the trick. Training sessions should be quite short at first, no more than a minute, and the environment should be free of distractions. You can gradually increase the length of sessions and invite other people to watch once Buttons has become more proficient. If, during a given session, he doesn't feel like working, walk him through the trick, and then reward him promptly.

Soothing words of praise, on the other hand, seem to be a more effective means of reinforcing spontaneous good behavior. Assuming you enjoy having your cat jump into your lap, praise him each time he does, and enhance your words with a few minutes of gentle scratching behind his ears or under his chin. You could even try your best to simulate a purr by exhaling forcefully through your mouth while fluttering your tongue against your hard palate. It is not recommended that you attempt this while anyone else is in the room, however.

Reprimands

Discouraging inappropriate behavior is often the most difficult aspect of training, largely because most people react to unpleasantness with anger or annoyance. The first rule of reprimand, then, is to remain calm. Do not scream. Do not tear your hair or gnash your teeth. Above all, do not beat or otherwise mistreat your cat. Physical abuse will only yield a disobedient cat who hates you. The only physical reproof a cat will accept is a light swat across the bottom or the snout — only because his mother did the same thing.

You can, however, forge an association between unacceptable behavior and danger. Though inherently brave, almost all cats instinctively shy away from two very simple things: loud noises and water. Both represent immediate threats to survival. Loud noises usually signal the approach of a larger, and potentially hungrier, predator. Water, meanwhile, poses a somewhat more complex problem. With the exception of certain breeds, cats are not very capable swimmers; whether they know this instinctively or learn through unhappy experience, most cats run from the merest suggestion of a dip.

Noise and water, therefore, are the most effective deterrents to inappropriate behavior. If you catch your cat doing something you don't like, try clapping your hands, or throwing an object such as a magazine or a book near the spot where he is misbehaving. Don't throw anything directly at your cat, as this will merely build an association between you and pain, and effectively undercut any attempt to train him. Likewise, don't throw anything that will shatter or break, since flying pieces may strike him. Alternatively, you may discourage him from clawing up your prize antimacassars by squirting him with water. Either a squirt gun or a spray bottle will serve quite effectively.

Whatever means you choose, accompany your reprimand with a firm, clear "No!" Soon enough, Felicity will associate "No!" with a jet of water or an unpleasant noise. In many cases, verbal reproof alone will discourage undesirable activities. Perhaps, in the same way soothing tones are understood as purring, an emphatic utterance is the human equivalent of a hiss or growl.

As with rewards, reprimands are usually effective only when immediately associated with the behavior that gives rise to them. It won't do much good to scold your cat for leaving paw prints on the counter if you notice his tracks hours after he's made them. You have to catch him in the act.

Problem Behaviors

Persistent wrongdoing, or inappropriate behavior that occurs while you're out of the room, require stronger measures. In most cases, these involve setting up some type of assuredly unpleasant consequence. Only in rare instances can you succeed in teaching your cat to forswear something he has done hours ago behind your back.

To inhibit certain activities such as clawing furniture, prancing across counters, or taking a leisurely afternoon nap on the dinner table, try setting a booby trap. (It is assumed you have already provided a scratching post and suitable areas for climbing and reclining.) Balance an aluminum pan or bowl, or a book, on a dowel close to the spot your cat regularly abuses; avoid using anything breakable. The next time Thumper leaps on his favorite chair or jumps on the counter, he will dislodge the stick and send the bowl clattering. Some people find balloons equally effective. Attach one to your cat's secret scratching place, and as he investigates this new feature of the landscape, sharp kitty claws will sooner or later produce an extremely unpleasant sound.

Chewing, or teething, requires a somewhat different approach. If your cat develops a habit of chewing electrical cords, for instance, rub Tabasco sauce on his gums. Make sure he really learns to hate the taste. Then coat your electric cords with it. Alternatively, you may coat them with a thin layer of petroleum jelly mixed with pepper. Rather than force your cat to ingest pepper, though, blow a few grains into his nose. Plain black pepper also works on objects that might otherwise be damaged. Plants may be sprayed with a mixture of water and white vinegar, lime juice, or lemon juice. As with Tabasco sauce, rub your cat's gums or nose with a tiny bit of the mixture before spraying your plants.

Dangling appliance cords may be smeared with Tabasco, or else rigged with a booby trap. Don't wait for the lamp to come crashing down; tie a string to the cord and attach the other end to an aluminum pan. When your cat starts playing with the cord, the attached string will pull down the pan.

Breaking litter box training is a more ticklish problem. More often than not, your cat has a good reason for soiling the carpet or the quilt. He may have a bladder infection or some other digestive tract problem; a trip to the vet is advised before exploring other reasons. Perhaps his box is dirtier than he prefers; perhaps the door to the bathroom has inadvertently been closed. The stress of traveling or boarding can cause loose stools. Cats left alone for an extended period may leave a nasty gift in the front hall to signal their unhappiness. Other times, they'll do so after being disciplined. If a newcomer — feline, human, or canine — arrives in his territory, a cat may leave a malodorous warning to prove his claim.

While every attempt should be made to discover the reason behind unexpected soiling, you must still reprimand your cat. The simplest way to do so is to soak a paper towel or dishrag with white vinegar and take it to the spot your cat has soiled. Then fetch your cat; don't bother trying to call him, because he won't come. Push his face close enough to the urine or feces so that he associates it with what's to come, then stick the soaked paper towel or rag under his nose. Let him go after he gets a good whiff, and after you clean the spot, pour a few drops of white vinegar on it. (White vinegar is preferred because it doesn't stain.)

If your cat repeats his bad behavior, have him examined by a vet. If the problem cannot be traced to any physical cause, you will have to confine your cat to the room where his litter box is located. Be sure to place his food and water as far away from the box as possible. After he has begun to use his box again, you can let him out while you are around to watch him. If he heads to the spot or spots he has previously soiled, throw a magazine or squirt him with water. If he persists, or soils another spot, start over with vinegar and confine him again.

Continue the procedure until he resumes regular use of his box. In rare instances — typically those involving an adult cat that has never been housebroken — the entire process may take more time than you might initially have anticipated, but it will come to an end. As has been noted earlier, cats are creatures of habit: They feel most comfortable doing what they've done before. More important, no matter how willful your cat may be, you are bigger, stronger, and ultimately, smarter.

Consistency

Like small children, cats will only behave well if you reward or reprimand them promptly and persistently. If you forget just once to hand over a treat after Misty shuffles off to Buffalo for your Uncle Wilbur, it's the last dance she'll ever do. Drop one scrap of chicken from the dinner table and Zach will stand in wait every night. "Just this once" does not correspond to anything a cat understands. Unlike humans, who seem to live their lives as though it were a dry run for something more rewarding, a cat plays everything for keeps. It's a lesson well worth learning.

TRAVEL

If you've read through the previous chapters of this book, you have no doubt grasped that cats do not like to be left alone for extended periods. Of course, one of the great advantages of cat ownership is that you can leave home for a weekend — provided you've left out an ample supply of dry food and water and made sure the litter box is scrupulously clean. If you're going to be away for three or more days, however, you will need to consider one of the following options:

- Have someone stop by or cat-sit
- Take your cat with you
- Board her

Should you neglect to take appropriate steps, you will at best cause your cat undue emotional stress. At worst, you may put her health, or her life, in jeopardy.

Leaving Your Cat Home

For short trips of a week or ten days, perhaps the simplest and most economical answer is to ask a friend or neighbor to check in once or twice a day to make sure the cat has enough food and the litter box is clean. The best home visits are made by people who really like cats, as they are most likely to give yours a bit more time and affection. Failing this, ask someone you know you can count on.

Of course, from your cat's point of view, the ideal solution is to arrange for someone to actually stay in your home. This will provide her with a more constant flow of attention and reassurance. In any case, always leave detailed instructions on care and feeding, and include any telephone numbers where you can be reached, as well as the phone number and address of your cat's doctor.

Taking Your Cat with You

Especially if accustomed to taking trips at a young age, most cats make steady travel companions. Even older, less experienced cats can learn to travel, if properly prepared for the journey.

Some cats actively enjoy taking trips; admittedly, they are rare exceptions to the general rule. Before setting off on a trip, you'll need to assemble the following items:

- A carrier or cage
- Newspaper or a towel to line the carrier
- Paper towels to clean up accidents
- A portable litter box
- Favorite toys
- Your cat's medical records
- Medications your cat regularly requires
- Dry and wet food
- A can opener
- Food and water bowls

If you'll be traveling by car for several days, you will also need to take along a bottle of water. No matter how unhappy he is about traveling, your cat will probably want to eat and drink something after five or six hours on the road — and will certainly want to polish off a bit of food when you stop for the night.

A few days before the trip, place the carrier or cage in the open, so your cat can get used to it. If he's traveled before, this will help to prepare him psychologically to expect a trip. On the day of departure, make sure the carrier is lined with newspaper. Spend a little extra cozy time together, if possible, but try not to feed him less than five hours before departure. This should give him time to digest and void his bowels.

You may wish to ask your veterinarian about tranquilizers. Don't automatically assume your cat will need them, as most cats do not enjoy mood-altering drugs. Many cats travel well without them, but some may find the trip so stressful they soil themselves, vomit, or yowl themselves hoarse. Under no circumstances may you give your cat medication prescribed for humans. Cats metabolize a variety of common substances far differently than humans; even aspirin can cause a severely toxic reaction. Only give your cat medications that have been authorized by a veterinarian, and only in the dosage prescribed.

Traveling by Car

If possible, allow some time before the trip to acquaint your cat with the fascinating experience of automobile travel. As mentioned above, leave the carrier out several days ahead of time. A day or two before the trip, put your cat in the carrier and take her out to the car, talking soothingly along the way; after a few minutes, bring her back inside. The next day, take her for one or two short rides.

For long automobile trips, you may prefer to use a cage instead of a carrier. This way, she can have access to her litter box and a small bowl of food at all times, and even move around a bit if the mood arises. In any event, for trips of three hours or more, you'll need to have a small, filled litter box in the car, a bottle of water, and a bowl.

If you plan on stopping along the way, make sure in advance that the motel or hotel allows pets. You can't leave a cat in the car when the sun is shining, since the temperature inside a vehicle can climb to 120 degrees in a matter of minutes, and your cat will suffer heatstroke. Nor can you leave her in the car on a cold day, since the temperature inside the vehicle will rapidly drop if the heat is not on. Don't even consider putting your cat in the trunk.

Public Transportation

Many public carriers will allow cats, if they are suitably contained. Amtrak, however, expressly prohibits pets, as do many interstate bus lines. Cruise ship policies vary, though even those lines that allow pets may insist that they travel in special kennel areas. All airlines require advance registration for pets, which typically involves a fee. Most require proof of certain vaccinations, particularly rabies. Only carriers that can fit under the seat are allowed in the passenger cabin, and some will only transport pets in the baggage compartment. This is not recommended for cats. Although strict temperature and air-quality guidelines have been established for areas in which animals are contained during flight, the noise is fairly horrendous. If your cat wasn't neurotic before the trip, she will be at the end of a voyage in the cargo compartment. Before making plans to use public transportation, therefore, always find out the company's policy.

Regulations concerning travel to certain islands or international destinations must also be investigated in advance. Many Caribbean islands do not allow cats at all, while Hawaii and Great Britain impose lengthy quarantines. Before setting off for an international adventure or island escape, check with your veterinarian, the airline or cruise line you're using, or the embassy or travel information bureau of the place you intend to visit.

Boarding

When you can't, or don't wish to, travel with your cat, and no one can look in on her, the only option is to arrange for care outside your home. The preferred setting would be the residence of someone who doesn't own cats or dogs, and who would enjoy looking after a temporary companion. If this person is known to your cat, so much the better.

Unfortunately, the preferred choice is not always available. In this case, you will have to arrange temporary lodgings at a cattery. Though some kennels will look after cats as well as dogs, a sojourn of any length in a strange environment — locked in a cage, never knowing if she will ever see her home and family again — is likely to cause your cat enough stress, without the added vexation of a lot of yapping and barking. She may stop eating or grow ill. She'll almost certainly find a way to punish you when you return.

In order to minimize her distress, make every effort to choose the most scrupulously operated facility you can find. Consult your veterinarian, and ask friends and acquaintances who own animals. Once you've collected a list of possibilities, visit each one, and evaluate them according to the following factors:

- General cleanliness
- Attitude of caregivers
- Temperature
- Absence of flies or other insects
- Physical and emotional well-being of animals
- Diet

You'll also need to find out if the management requires proof of vaccinations prior to boarding. Even if proof is not required, for the sake of your cat's health, you'll want to be sure she is current on all vaccinations.

When you drop her off at a cattery or kennel, leave emergency contact information — including your telephone numbers, your vet's, and those of friends or relatives who can act on your behalf should the need arise. If allowed, bring some of her toys, a piece or two of your clothing for her to sleep with, and her litter box. When you pick her up after your trip, make sure you have a box or can of her favorite treats on hand. She may reject both you and the treats at first, but with time and patience she will probably forgive you.

Moving

There's no way to communicate adequately to your cat the positive aspects of changing residence. All she can see are the cherished landmarks of her territory disappearing one by one into boxes. She'll probably sense your fatigue after a long day of packing, and your nervousness as the date looms closer. The day of the actual move is filled with confusion, herds of strangers pounding across the floors, and a host of strange, new scents and sounds.

You can ease the transition somewhat by giving Boo some extra affection and allowing her to investigate the boxes you're packing. On the day of the move, keep her confined with her litter box, toys, and dishes in a room the movers will not have to enter. If this isn't possible, keep her in her cage or carrier in an area least accessible to traffic.

If possible, take her to your new residence after the move has been completed, and set her in a quiet room along with all of her necessary and most valued possessions. Failing this, place her carrier as before in an area where she is least likely to be disturbed. Over the next few weeks, while you're unpacking and ordering your new home, try to confine her to a single room along with her things. Once your new abode is settled, place the litter box and food dishes where you want them, and introduce your cat to their new locations — just as you did when you first brought her home. Afterward, let her explore her new territory at will.

You may find that she has an accident or two after a move. It's likely the result of stress, though she may simply have become disoriented and forgotten the location of the litter box. No matter how sorry you feel for her, you must reprimand her after an accident. Give her an hour, and then show her where the litter box has been moved. In her heart of hearts, she is just as anxious to start life in her new home on the right foot as you are.

GROOMING

A healthy, happy cat spends a substantial part of every day grooming himself. Cleanliness is not his only aim, however. In cold weather, for instance, smooth fur provides better insulation. On hot days, depositing saliva through licking helps to lower overall body temperature. Sunlight, meanwhile, produces vitamin D on the coat, so after a nice nap in the sun, a cat will groom himself to ingest this important nutrient.

Cats will also groom themselves when anxious or puzzled, the same way people scratch their heads. They'll also lick their fur in order to reestablish their own scent after being held or stroked, or after coming into contact with a foreign object or animal. Finally, vigorous grooming stimulates glands at the base of every hair, which produce tiny secretions of oil that protect the fur from water and other loathsome substances.

Still, most cats appreciate a little extra help. Long-haired breeds positively require assistance; but regularly brushing or combing any cat can significantly reduce the likelihood he'll vomit up a dreaded hair ball. It will also inhibit fuzzy buildup on furniture and floors. Most important, a little time devoted to grooming will deepen the bonds of affection between you and your cat — especially when you brush out those hard-to-reach areas behind his ears.

Long-Haired Cats

To groom a long-haired cat, you'll need:

- A steel comb with wide-tooth and narrow-tooth sections
- A fine-tooth, or flea comb
- A natural fiber grooming brush

Before commencing, it's usually a good idea to run your fingers through your cat's coat. Not only will this allow you to check for tangles or matted areas, it will also relax the cat.

Begin by running the wide-tooth portion of the steel comb downward through the fur along your cat's head, back, sides, and tail. Proceed next to his chin and chest. Finally, while holding him against your chest and supporting his front paws with your free hand, gently comb his stomach, the inside of the legs, and under the tail. Use your fingers to divide tangles into smaller bundles before easing the comb through; otherwise, you're liable to end up with a nasty bite or claw mark. If for some reason the coat is badly matted, you'll probably need to take Rex to the vet, where he'll be tranquilized and clipped.

Next, repeat the entire process using the narrow-tooth portion of the comb. You can enhance the pleasure of the experience by talking to your cat, reciting poetry, or singing some of the old songs you both know and love so well. Once you've finished the second combing, you're ready to fluff. Lightly brush the fur around his neck and chest forward and away from his body, and then do the same to the tail. A light once-over in a downward direction over the rest of his coat will add luster. Finally, use the flea comb to groom the delicate fur around his face and ears.

From time to time, you may discover fecal matter clinging to the fur underneath your cat's tail. This rather inelegant detail is rarely mentioned in descriptions of longhairs, but it's a common problem. The simplest procedure, if you're not going to show your cat, is to clip the area under the tail. Otherwise, you will have to wash the offending material away instantly upon discovery.

Short-Haired Cats

Most cats shed during fall and spring, and dry heat during the winter months can lead to off-season molting. Shorthairs thus benefit from weekly or semiweekly attention. The process is obviously simpler and quicker than grooming a longhair. In most instances, running a fine-tooth or flea comb lightly over the entire body will remove dead hair. If your cat likes the sensation, you may finish up with a rubber brush. Avoid applying too much pressure, though; overzealous brushing can pull out too much hair, leaving bald patches that will embarrass you and your cat.

Bathing

Short-haired cats who don't come into contact with potentially flea-bearing animals will generally not need to be bathed. Exceptions occur from time to time, of course: an accident with potting soil, perhaps, or a vigil among the dust bunnies. However, cats with long or semilong fur are apt to attract dirt, dust, or other unseemly substances, and will require more than occasional bathing. Many shampoos, specific to certain types of coats, are available in pet stores. Should your cat have fleas, consult your veterinarian before purchasing flea shampoo, as some brands may be too harsh for your cat, while others are formulated only for dogs. If at all possible, take your cat to a professional groomer for bathing. With the exception of Turkish Angoras and Abyssinians, cats almost universally despise water; and even the exceptional breeds can't always be counted on to live up to their reputations.

If you must bathe the cat yourself, wear clothing that protects your arms and legs, and slip on some rubber gloves. A hat with a veil, however, is probably excessive. In a room free from drafts, fill a sink or laundry tub halfway with lukewarm water, and set several towels within easy reach. Prior to introducing your cat to the tub, wash her face and ears with a washcloth sprinkled with a few drops of shampoo, and rinse by wiping several times with warm water. Finally, lower her gently into the tub, holding her front paws with one hand and supporting her lower body with the other. Don't simply plop her in, and never dunk her head under water.

While she's screeching and clawing in a frantic effort to escape, wet her coat thoroughly, avoiding her face, eyes, and ears. The real fun begins when you apply the shampoo, which must be worked into a full lather; this may take some time, depending on how hard your cat struggles. Rinse all traces of lather with a sink hose or plastic cup, then use your hands to wring or wipe as much water out of the coat as you can. With any luck, your cat will be exhausted by this point, or at the very least grateful to be removed from the tub. Wrap a towel around her and blot her firmly, but gently. Avoid rubbing long-haired cats, as this may tangle their fur. Blot again, using a fresh towel.

Some cats don't mind being blow-dried; others object to the noise. If yours consents to this further indignity, always test the heat on your own skin, and adjust the temperature so that it doesn't burn. If she does not willingly submit, blot her with a third towel and confine her to a room absolutely free of drafts. It's a good idea, anyway, to keep doors and windows closed until the cat is completely dry — which, in the case of certain long-haired breeds, may take as long as twenty-four hours. When she is at least partially dry, give her a few treats (she'll be too busy licking herself before this point); afterward, give her a few more. While she will probably never associate bathing with pleasurable rewards, an extra show of concern on your part will help her to forgive.

Nail Trimming

Though your cat may divest himself of dead claw husks by scratching and gnawing, he can't actually trim his claws. This often becomes painfully evident when he jumps onto your lap or makes a lunge for your feet under the covers. Somewhat less obvious is the clicking noise his nails make as he walks across a bare floor; it will sound like a tiny dance troupe rehearsing a tap routine.

Nail trimming is your job. A cat that has had his nails trimmed since childhood will usually bear up more serenely than an older cat undergoing the process for the first time. In any case, wear protective clothing. If your cat puts up a serious fight, try trimming one or two nails per session. You may need to keep a chart so you remember which nails have already been trimmed.

The most effective tool is a pair of special clippers, available at most pet stores. Hold the cat on your lap, and gently press the pad of each toe until the claw is extended. Notice the red streak running through most of the claw; this is a vein, and will cause immense pain if cut, so be careful to trim only the transparent tip of the nail.

BREEDING

Sooner or later, all kittens grow up. According to the way of all flesh, they will seek to become fruitful and multiply. In feline societies, multiplication can occur at an astonishing rate indeed. Unrestrained, a female can give birth to two or even three litters per year, with an average of four kittens per litter. Assuming half of her kittens are female, this would represent an astronomical increase of the feline population in five years' time.

Nature usually begins to call male cats between the ages of eight to twelve months. Rarely does this occur earlier, though late bloomers are somewhat more common. Sexual maturity is accompanied by an unpleasant behavior known as "spraying," which involves staining vertical surfaces with a particularly strong-smelling urine, the scent of which is all but impossible to eradicate. He will also become restive, pacing and possibly howling around the house, like a troubled adolescent in a 1950s melodrama.

Females awaken somewhat earlier, usually between six and twelve months; though some have been known to suffer pangs of desire as early as three to five months. Signs of maturity include insistent yowling or meowing, rolling on the floor, rubbing amorously against legs and furniture, and assuming a crouched position with her tail bent to one side and her back arched high. This condition is commonly referred to as "being in heat," and continues night and day anywhere from a week to ten days, and often longer.

Faced with these challenging transformations of personality, the average cat owner has two choices. If your cat is pedigreed, you may wish to breed him or her, in which case you will have to put up with unruly behavior for some time. If the animal is not pedigreed, or if you don't wish to breed your cat, you can have it neutered. These are your only options. Should you neglect your responsibility, either through well-meaning "naturalism" or sheer laziness, life with your cat will become a waking nightmare.

Pedigree Breeding

Before embarking on an adventure of this sort, consider well whether your cat is truly an exquisite example of its breed, and whether you have the time, money, and stamina to see the project through to its completion. Another factor worth contemplating is whether or not your area represents a large enough market for the breed.

If your cat is female, you will have to locate a stud for her. Stud service is usually fee-based, and the owner will probably ask to examine your cat's pedigree and show history (if any). Moreover, because males prefer to mate on their own turf, you will have to bring your female to him. Sometimes, the anxiety of relocation to foreign territory may cause your female to go out of heat. Stud service should therefore be governed by written contract, in case complications of this or any other sort arise.

If your cat is male, you may decide to offer stud service. While this entails less work than caring for a pregnant mother, assisting in raising her litter, and finding suitable homes for each kitten, it's no easy matter to temporarily board a female in heat. In addition, you will have to find a way to cope with a male who sprays your furniture, guests, and family members.

Neutering

The idea of interfering with a cat's reproductive integrity may seem objectionable at first. Ultimately, however, it is kinder than letting nature take her course. Nonneutered males may become permanently irritable. In females, the stress of repetitive heat cycles may lead to complications such as ovarian cysts, urinary tract infections, and madness.

Neutering is a fairly simple veterinary procedure. For males, it involves surgical removal of the testicles from the sac. Females undergo removal of the ovaries and all or part of the uterus; this is often referred to as "spaying." Both procedures require anesthesia, so you mustn't feed your cat the day before the operation; following surgery, an overnight stay at the clinic or veterinarian's office is also required.

Males usually recover very quickly after neutering. You may have to make a few dietary adjustments, however, because a strictly or predominantly dry food diet can cause problems in the urinary tract. Females tend to heal more slowly: Spaying is a more invasive procedure, and the recovery period typically lasts about a week. As with any surgical procedure, monitor your cat's behavior carefully. If swelling or infection develops, or your cat seems listless, refuses to use the litter box, or gnaws persistently at the stitches, contact your vet immediately.

The cost of neutering depends on the type of facility where the operation is performed. A number of adoption facilities offer low-cost or even free neutering, and local clinics may also offer a low rate. Private practice veterinarians usually charge a somewhat higher fee, though in return your pet will likely receive more attentive observation and aftercare. Since spaying involves more complex surgery than castration, it's almost invariably more expensive.

An organization known as Friends of Animals may be able to direct you to a low-cost neutering facility in your area. They may also make reduced-rate certificates available, which a private practice veterinarian in your area may accept. Friends of Animals may be reached at 1-800-321-7387.

HEALTH CARE

Cats are generally hardy animals, and if you are wise enough to keep them indoors, you may never have to deal with a feline illness of a serious nature. Naturally, you will take your cat for an initial veterinary examination within a week of adoption; and the veterinarian will examine coat, eyes, and ears, administer vaccinations, set up a booster schedule, and test for the presence of various deadly diseases, such as feline leukemia and feline AIDS.

Still, accidents of various sorts can occur during your cat's lifetime, and minor illnesses may lay him low for brief periods. Home examinations, as well as a basic familiarity with certain symptoms, should alert you to potential health problems. Should your cat appear ill or suffer an accident, always contact his doctor. A cat can't tell you where something hurts or why, and if you ignore his problem for even a day or two in hopes that it will magically disappear, you may seriously jeopardize his life.

Basic Home Care

A simple, routine examination of the major parts of your cat's body can help you keep track of his health and development. The checkup may easily be performed along with grooming or nail clipping; in addition to alerting you to signs of disease or infection, a regular examination can help fine-tune your cat's appearance. Typically, five areas should be checked at least once a week.

Teeth. Kittens usually have a full set of milk teeth by the age of three weeks. By five months, these will be replaced by permanent teeth, and the milk teeth will either be swallowed or spat out. From this point onwards, inspect your cat's teeth for tartar, which often builds up as a result of a steady diet of wet food. Light buildup may be handled by introducing a bit of dry food into your cat's diet (only about an eighth of a cup per day for neutered males). Heavier accretions will have to be scraped by a veterinarian. In addition, vivid red lines on the gum around the teeth may herald gingivitis, which is usually accompanied by particularly foul breath. Your veterinarian will need to treat the condition.

Anus. Long-haired cats are prone to accretions of fecal matter in the region just below the tail. Heavy deposits on short-haired cats, and persistent coating of the anal region among longhairs, usually indicates diarrhea. Check the litter box for soft or runny stools.

Diarrhea may be caused by a number of different factors — including emotional distress, parasites, and viral infection. If symptoms persist for several days, contact your veterinarian.

Skin and Coat. The coat should feel full and soft, and its appearance is usually glossy. Constant scratching or licking at a particular spot, bald patches, and prodigious shedding usually indicate an infestation or infection. Ringworm, for example, tends to produces bare patches that are sometimes scaly or crusty, while fleas or other parasites can cause itching and painful inflammations. Cuts or slashes may become infected. Any change in coat, skin, or grooming behavior should be reported to the veterinarian.

Eyes and Nose. Spots of dried mucus — colloquially known as "sleep" — may appear in the corners of your cat's eyes. You may wipe these away with a moist tissue or cotton ball, or a clean fingertip. Crusty deposits at the outer edges of the nostrils may be similarly wiped away. Persistent tearing, or eyes coated with mucus, signal an infection or the presence of a foreign body in the eye, and require prompt veterinary attention. Likewise, a runny nose (usually accompanied by sneezing and a tendency to breathe through the mouth) may be a symptom of a viral or bacterial infection.

Ears. Regular inspection of the ears may reveal small deposits of dirt or other objectionable matter, which may be removed with a slightly damp tissue or cotton ball. Never use a cotton swab to clean your cat's ears, and never insert anything into the ear canal. If your cat persistently shakes his head and scratches at his ears, and inspection reveals smeary dark deposits and brown crusts inside the ear, he has mites, and must be taken promptly to the veterinarian.

In addition to checking these areas, keep an eye out for other signs of illness. Symptoms include:

- General listlessness (what your mother called "droopiness")
- Difficulty walking
- Labored breathing
- Persistent coughing or vomiting
- Lack of coordination
- Failure to respond to sounds or movement
- Frequent or persistent soiling
- Inability to urinate, or painful urination

If your cat manifests any of these symptoms, contact your veterinarian immediately.

Vaccinations and Testing

Kittens who drink their mother's milk within twenty-four hours of birth are typically protected against diseases for which their mother has received vaccinations. "First milk," or colostrum, contains a unique combination of proteins and antibodies that temporarily immunize a kitten for about fourteen to sixteen weeks. Before this period ends, kittens should be vaccinated against various diseases.

Vaccination is essential to prevent occurrence of a variety of respiratory illnesses, panleucopenia (an intestinal virus more commonly known as distemper), rabies, and feline leukemia. In addition, a relatively new vaccine has been developed for Feline Infectious Peritonitis (FIP), although its safety and effectiveness is still being debated. In order to develop immunities, kittens should receive initial vaccinations at about eight weeks old, and boosters according to a schedule determined by your veterinarian. The following table represents a typical vaccination and booster schedule:

VACCINATION AND BOOSTER SCHEDULE

Age	Respiratory Diseases	Distemper	Leukemia	Rabies	FIP
8 weeks	✔	✔	✔		
12 weeks	✔	✔	✔		
16 weeks				✔	✔
19 weeks				✔	✔

Thereafter, a booster once a year is recommended for most vaccines; some states require rabies boosters only once every three years. If you're planning to board or travel with your cat, check the facility's, state's, or country's policy on rabies well in advance.

In addition, if you've adopted an adult cat or an older kitten and do not have his medical records, don't automatically assume he's had his shots. Discuss the situation with your vet when you bring your cat in for his first visit. Your vet will probably advise a complete vaccination series.

Common Diseases

Cats allowed to ramble outdoors face a high risk of contracting a fatal illness or unpleasant parasitic infestation. Yet even indoor cats may develop serious health problems. In some cases, a virus may be transmitted by a new cat introduced into the home, or else by intermediate carriers — including people, clothing, or another cat's toys. In other cases, the cause is internal. Like humans, cats carry a number of viruses and bacterial strains in their systems from birth; and some cats seem to be inherently better at resisting these pathogens than others.

Vaccination, cleanliness, and restriction to the indoors constitute the best defense against disease. Still, it's beneficial to have a basic understanding of the most common ailments. At the very least, you'll know what you're up against, and why.

Respiratory Illness. Upper respiratory ailments are most often caused by feline herpes virus type 1 (FHV-1), feline calicivirus (FCV), and chlamydia. FHV and FCV typically produce cold or flulike symptoms, include sneezing, runny nose, fever, conjunctivitis, and corneal or oral ulcers. Treatment usually requires a broad spectrum antibiotic. The most common symptom of chlamydia is conjunctivitis, which is often treated with a topical antibiotic ointment in addition to oral antibiotics. Vaccines for all three diseases are generally included in the standard series of inoculations. Owners handling a cat suffering from chlamydia must scrupulously clean their hands and any other exposed body parts, as the bacterial infection is communicable to humans.

Panleucopenia (Distemper). This severe viral infection can be transmitted through contact with other cats or through contact with someone or something that has come into contact with an infected cat. Symptoms include vomiting, diarrhea, fever, and depression; infection will also impair production of white blood cells. Since the disease intensifies rapidly, swift treatment is absolutely essential. Vaccination provides effective protection, if repeated annually. And as your mother probably warned you, always wash your hands after handling a strange cat.

Rabies. Rabies is a fatal disease, usually transmitted through the bite of an infected animal. However, the virus can also be transmitted through licking, scratching, or contact with feces. The incubation period can last anywhere from several days to two years, before the virus reaches the brain and symptoms develop. The first symptoms are usually behavioral. A rabid cat will often stop eating and drinking, and seek solitude. As the disease progresses, the cat may either become gradually paralyzed, beginning with the throat and jaw, or else they will turn vicious, attacking anything in their path and snapping at imaginary creatures or objects. Once symptoms appear, death follows within three days to a week. Rabies can be transmitted to humans, even when the infected animal shows no symptoms. It is imperative to protect yourself and anyone with whom your cat comes in contact through vaccination.

Feline Urinary Syndrome (FUS). FUS covers a wide range of symptoms arising from inflamed, irritated, or obstructed urinary tracts. Males are much more likely than females to suffer from FUS. Among females, symptoms may include difficulty urinating, appearance of blood in the urine, frequent trips to the litter box, and breaking litter box training. In addition to these symptoms, males may experience blockage in the urethra, making it impossible to urinate. The signs of obstruction include persistent, fruitless attempts at urination, howling, distended bladder, depression, vomiting, diarrhea, dehydration, and loss of appetite. Left untreated, obstruction will rapidly lead to uremic poisoning and death. If FUS is recognized in time, most cats can go on to lead happy, productive lives. Treatment may include dietary changes, catheterization, or surgery. In addition, your cat must be watched closely for any signs of recurrence.

Feline Leukemia (FeLV). The feline leukemia virus weakens a cat's immune system. Extremely contagious, the virus spreads from cat to cat via saliva, blood, and urine, and possibly from a mother to her unborn kittens. Any object a cat shares with other cats — including bowls, litter boxes, and toys — may become likely sources of transmission, as can grooming or bite wounds. Immune impairment through FeLV most often causes anemia, but substantially increases the risk of cancer, and bacterial and viral infections. Obvious symptoms depend largely on the type of secondary infection, but many cats manifest a chronic wasting, sluggishness, and poor appetite. Lung infections and mouth sores are also common in cats infected with the virus. While testing for FeLV is common, there is, unfortunately, no cure.

Feline AIDS (FIV). FIV is related to the same category of immune-suppressant viruses as HIV. It is passed among cats most typically through bites or open wounds. It cannot be transmitted to humans, nor can humans pass the virus on to cats. However, FIV-positive cats must be kept indoors at all times, and away from other cats. Like FeLV, FIV cripples the immune system, so an infected cat becomes susceptible to a wide variety of secondary illness, all of which are difficult to fight. The most common problems are chronic oral infections and respiratory problems, although roughly twenty percent of all infected cats suffer chronic stomach ailments and diarrhea. In recent years, FIV testing has become standard among veterinarians. Like FeLV, however, there is no cure.

Feline Infectious Peritonitis (FIP). Because no test is yet available to determine whether a cat has been exposed to FIP virus, only a biopsy can positively identify the virus. The exact method of transmission has not been determined either, though it is highly likely to be passed through the saliva, urine, and feces of an infected animal. The disease typically occurs in one of two forms: wet, in which the abdomen and chest cavity fill with fluid, impairing breathing; and dry, in which little or no fluid accumulates. Symptoms of dry FIP include loss of coordination, partial or complete paralysis of the back legs, convulsions, personality changes, and impairment or loss of vision. Although treatment may temporarily relieve symptoms, there is no cure for FIP.

Allergies. Like people, cats may suffer a wide range of allergic reactions. Some may be allergic to airborne particles, such as cigarette smoke, perfumes, and pollen. Food allergies and allergic reaction to certain medications, such as antibiotics or anesthesia, usually result in nausea, vomiting, diarrhea, and appetite loss. Topical allergies may result from prolonged contact with certain oily types of plants, wool, dust, newsprint, and cleaning materials. Typical symptoms include skin inflammations or pigment changes.

Internal Parasites

Parasites are nasty little creatures that feed off the tissues of larger living organisms. Internal parasites typically burrow inside a cat's digestive tract, causing unpleasant symptoms at best, and serious health problems at worst. Many will happily transfer accommodations from your cat's body onto yours, should the opportunity arise.

Worms are the most common type of internal parasites, and include several varieties:

Roundworms live in the intestines, and feed off of digesting food. Symptoms include diarrhea, constipation, anemia, potbellies, general lethargy. Kittens can die from a serious infestation. Larvae may migrate into the tissues of children's skin. Young children should therefore be kept from soiled cat litter, and cats should not be allowed to play in children's sandboxes.

Hookworms may enter your cat's body either through the mouth or the skin. While rarely affecting humans, hookworms can cause severe anemia in cats, because they live off blood sucked from the intestine walls. Symptoms include diarrhea (which may contain blood) and lethargy.

Tapeworms are usually transmitted through a secondary host, usually fleas. So if your cat has fleas, or has suffered an infestation, he may very well have tapeworms. The head of the worm attaches itself to the intestinal lining, while other parts, which contain eggs, break off and are passed through feces. These parts resemble small grains of white rice, and are easy to identify around the anus and in stool samples.

Whipworms and Threadworms are less common. While the first type infest the large intestine, the latter lodge in the small. Both may cause diarrhea, anemia, and internal bleeding.

If you suspect your cat has worms, avoid using over-the-counter remedies. You will probably not diagnose the infestation correctly, and you may not administer the proper dosage. Since worm remedies are toxic, a mistake can wreak more havoc on your poor cat's health. Instead, take your cat, along with a fresh stool sample, to the veterinarian. In addition to providing the proper medication, your vet can advise you how to prevent subsequent infestations.

Toxoplasmosis is an extremely dangerous infection caused by a single-cell internal parasite that lodges in the cat's intestines. Eggs are passed through a cat's feces, and mature within a few days. Invisible to the naked eye, the eggs may be easily transferred to human hands during litter box cleaning, and later ingested. It is therefore essential to scoop the litter box daily, and wash your hands thoroughly with soap and hot water immediately after contact with litter or stool. Pregnant women are especially advised not to go near the litter box, as infection may cause fetal brain or eye damage; in addition, they should be tested for existing infection as soon as they learn they are pregnant. While the parasite is often passed through stool, it is more commonly ingested in raw or undercooked meat. For the sake of your own health and your cat's, freshly killed birds or mice — or any type of raw meat — should be stricken from the menu.

External Parasites

These beasts embed themselves in a cat's coat or skin. Most forms are easy to manage, though given half a chance, they'll leap from Fluffy to you before you can scream. If you wish to avoid embarrassing fits of scratching and twitching, take care of an infestation as soon as it develops. The most common external parasites are:

Fleas are tiny brown jumping creatures that burrow in your cat's fur and suck blood from his skin. They move faster than jack rabbits, and breed even more rapidly. A bath using special flea shampoo, followed by frequent powdering or spraying of the cat's body, will usually kill fleas and eggs living on your cat. Twice-daily combing with a flea comb may serve as an additional — but not alternative — treatment. You'll also have to annihilate the intruders that must surely have migrated to other parts of your home. Fleas and flea eggs can live for more than a year in bedding, carpets, and cracks in the floor. Bombs, sprays, or powders are usually effective, though in cases of severe infestation, a professional exterminator may have to be engaged. Before using any chemical compound, however, always consult your veterinarian. Some flea preparations may be too strong for certain cats.

Lice, like fleas, cause intense itching, but are somewhat easier to control using flea powders or sprays. Adults resemble small grains of rice; eggs look like dandruff.

Ticks fasten themselves to a cat's skin, particularly around the ears and toes. The surest way to remove these brutes is to pluck them off individually. First, dab each tick with rubbing alcohol to paralyze it; then use tweezers to pull it off, and drop it in a jar of alcohol. Don't use excessive force to remove the tick, as the head may remain embedded in your cat's skin. If it seems to resist, dab it with more alcohol. Afterward, wash all affected areas to prevent your cat from licking the alcohol. Certain types of deer ticks carry Lyme disease, which can be seriously debilitating and sometimes fatal; the size of a pinhead, deer ticks are difficult to see. If your cat has become infested, you must consult both your doctor and your veterinarian.

Mites of different varieties can cause itching and other uncomfortable symptoms. The most common type are ear mites, which produce a black discharge inside the ear. All types are contagious, however. They may be destroyed through several applications of insecticide.

Administering Medication

As part of the treatment, your veterinarian may prescribe certain medications to be given once or several times daily. Some cats patiently allow you to give them foul-tasting drops or pills; most make quite a production out of it. Attempts to disguise medication in food do not usually succeed, and never more than once.

Few events in life are as disheartening as staring down at a bowl licked clean except for a tiny red pill in the center.

In general, it is easier to administer liquid medication than solid forms. Simply hold your cat's head with one hand while using your finger to hold his lower jaw down. Insert the end of the dropper into his mouth, squeeze the rubber end, remove the tube and hold your cat's mouth shut for a few seconds to make sure he's swallowed.

Unfortunately, most medication is prescribed in pill form, and will require somewhat more ingenuity and dexterity to ensure it's digested. Cats have a notorious habit of holding a pill in the side of their mouths and surreptitiously spitting it out as soon they slink out of sight. To administer a pill, tilt his head slightly backward and open his jaw as before. Drop the pill deep into the mouth, and then hold his jaw firmly shut while you gently rub his throat to engage his swallowing reflex. Afterward, tap him lightly on the nose. If he licks it, he's swallowed the pill.

Intravenous or subcutaneous injections, which may be necessary for certain illnesses such as diabetes or chronic renal failure, require detailed instruction by a veterinarian. Never try to give a cat a shot without proper instruction, as you may hurt your cat or deposit the medication in the wrong area. In addition, a chronically ill cat may require specialized medical devices. Proper training in the use of these devices is essential to prevent damage that may further complicate your cat's health.

Emergency Care

Finally, in case of accident, injury, or other emergency, you may need to take immediate steps to handle the situation until you can bring your cat to a hospital or veterinarian's office. Injured cats are often frightened, and may be uncooperative or aggressive when approached; some may attempt to run, or will scratch and bite anyone who tries to help them. Nevertheless, timely action may mean the difference between life and death.

As a precaution, it's a good idea to keep a first-aid kit in a convenient, easy-to-find location. The kit should include:

- Scissors
- Tape
- Bandages
- String or rope
- A blanket or thick towel, to be used for restraint or cases of severe bleeding or shock
- Hydrogen peroxide (to induce vomiting)
- Antibiotic ointments (for eyes and skin)

Also, make sure you know the location and telephone number of the nearest animal hospital or clinic that offers twenty-four-hour emergency service. The address and phone number should be clearly written out in the same location as your veterinarian's number.

The most likely emergency situations you are likely to face include:

Heatstroke. If a cat is confined to a car or cage exposed to direct sunlight, she may become groggy or unconscious, experience trouble breathing, or become severely agitated. It is essential to bring her body temperature down as quickly as possible, which may be effectively accomplished by dipping her in a tub or sink of cool water or soaking her with a hose. Immediately afterward, wrap her in a towel and transport her to the nearest vet or clinic.

Bleeding. Cuts or gashes may cause profuse bleeding, which may be controlled by the application of a pressure bandage. If nothing of the sort is available, wrap a clean sock or towel over the wound, or layer the area with paper towels; then wrap an adhesive bandage or a length of rope or string around the makeshift padding. If the bleeding is severe, wrap the cat in a towel before transporting her to the vet or clinic; this will help to prevent shock, and absorb blood.

Embedded Objects. Hooks, thorns, needles, pins, and other sharp objects may become embedded in your cat's paws. Do not attempt to remove objects that are deeply lodged in the flesh, as these can only be removed when the cat is sedated or anesthetized. If the object is only superficially embedded, you may attempt to remove it using tweezers or a sewing needle. Be prepared for strong objections on your cat's part, however. If you succeed in removing the object, bandage the afflicted area, and bring your cat to the vet, so she can be treated for an inevitable infection.

Fractures and Shock. If your cat falls from a very high place, is hit by a moving vehicle, or gets caught by a slamming door, he may suffer broken bones, and will probably go into shock. In particular, broken legs must be immobilized promptly, to minimize damage that might occur to blood vessels, nerves, and tendons. Wrap a towel, several washcloths, or several layers of newspaper or paper towel around the fracture, fix the layers in place with tape, string, or rope. Wrap the cat in towels or blankets to conserve body heat, and transport the animal to a hospital or emergency facility.

Swallowed Objects. In general, anything small enough to swallow will pass through the cat's body without causing harm. Sharp objects, such as needles, tacks, pins, or earring backs, may puncture the lining of the digestive tract, however. To cushion the object along the way, feed your cat small bits of cotton soaked in milk, and contact your veterinarian to discuss further steps.

Poisoning. Cats can easily become poisoned through grooming fur that has come into contact with a toxic substance. Plant nibbling and accidental ingestion of human medications are also common causes. If your cat has come into contact with a toxic substance such as cleaning solutions, paint, tar, or antifreeze, wash it off with soap and warm water before your cat has a chance to lick it off. Use soap and water or give it a complete bath in lukewarm (not cold) water. If you don't catch your cat in time, you may need to induce vomiting. The most effective methods involve giving one-quarter teaspoon of hydrogen peroxide (three percent solution) every ten minutes for half an hour, or one teaspoon of syrup of Ipecac per ten pounds of body weight. Don't attempt to induce vomiting if your cat has swallowed an acid, alkali, solvent, heavy-duty cleaner, petroleum product, medication, or any type of sharp object; shows symptoms of lethargy or appears comatose; or has swallowed the substance more than two hours prior to the onset of symptoms. You may attempt to coat the digestive tract with milk, egg whites, or vegetable oil; however, it is essential to check the label of any toxic substance to make sure these things will not react adversely. In all cases of poisoning, bring your cat to an emergency clinic or hospital as soon as possible.

Transporting Ill or Injured Cats

If possible, when moving an injured or severely ill animal, hold him by the skin of the neck and the rump and slide him gently onto a blanket or into a box with its side folded down. Avoid all unnecessary movements that may shift its backbone, legs, or tail. Once you have transferred the animal to a box, wrap him in blankets to keep him warm and minimize shifting; then transfer the box to your car.

Obviously, this procedure is easier to accomplish if the cat is unconscious or dazed. If he's conscious, keep talking to him every step of the way, as the sound of your voice will reassure him. If he puts up a fight, his condition is probably not too serious. Try and get him into his carrier; if he resists, force may aggravate his condition. Ultimately, you may have to let him lie or sit comfortably in the car with you, while you drive — cautiously — to the veterinarian's office or clinic.

IN SUM

The material in this chapter may sound ominously complex; the latter sections, in particular, may provoke undue anxiety in the reader. Please be assured that life with a cat is more often than not a simple affair. Complications and serious illnesses are rare if you take proper safety precautions inside your home and never let your cat outdoors. Regular visits to the veterinarian will also help to keep your pet in the bloom of health for many years to come. Still, forewarned is forearmed. If the potential hazards and complications of all relationships could be described in a handbook, the world would be a vastly calmer place. Fortunately, for the sake of artists and divorce lawyers everywhere, few associations are as simple — or as pleasant — as those between cats and people.

CHAPTER 7

Last Words

As mentioned in the first chapter, it is not unusual for a healthy cat to live as long as eighteen or twenty years. The idea tends to have a sobering effect on many people. Twenty years seems a rather lengthy commitment to a creature that, after all, can't do much to provide for you in your declining years. Even fourteen years, the average age of an indoor cat, is enough time for all the cells in your own body to completely regenerate themselves — twice. Yet, as their cat's journey through this life rounds to a close, few owners can honestly say their primary sensation has been one of relief.

Despite his unpredictability, his willfulness, and his sudden fits of passion, your cat will likely be a constant in your life. Unlike nearly every other creature you'll meet, he won't suddenly surprise you one morning by showing you a side of himself that is completely out of character. He will remain exactly what he is: a reliable mystery, an utterly self-contained individual. A cat.

AGING

It's estimated that during the first year of life, a cat ages roughly fifteen years in human terms. Thereafter, each year of his life is the equivalent of four years of human life. Measured in human years, a fourteen-year-old cat would be sixty-seven, while a twenty-year-old cat has reached the ripe old age of ninety-one.

Aging produces gradual changes in a cat's body, just as it does in a person's. At five years, your cat's metabolism has already begun to slow down a bit. You may notice slight personality changes typically associated with entering one's prime. He may seem less lively or more attached to his routine. He may develop a spare tire around his middle. Once your cat has reached middle age, attention to exercise and diet becomes necessary to maintain optimum health. It's up to you to goad him into staying in shape, perhaps by chasing him down the hall a few times a day, or going a couple of lively rounds of Run Around the Sofa, or carpet wrestling. His heart will thank you for it, and probably, so will yours.

By age ten, his system may show signs of slowing down even further. A gradual degeneration of his thyroid, adrenal glands, pancreas, and kidneys may lead to age-related complications such as chronic renal failure, hyperthyroidism, or diabetes. He may become more susceptible to respiratory diseases, and more sensitive to changes in temperature. It is therefore essential to maintain a schedule of annual or semiannual veterinary exams, in order to detect any underlying conditions and receive all necessary vaccination boosters.

Special Needs of Older Cats

As your cat sails into his golden years, physical and behavioral changes become more apparent. Symptoms may include:

- Cloudy eyes
- Thinning coat
- Prominent bones
- Loose skin

- Stiff joints and muscles
- Weakened senses
- Susceptibility to illness
- Excessive consumption of water or other fluids

He may become cranky and less accepting of changes in his environment. He may nod off in the middle of a conversation, or fall asleep before the nighttime news. He may pad around the house complaining.

Diet

Many mature cats lose their sense of smell. As this tends to manifest itself in a reduced appetite, strong-smelling food may be needed to lure Buttons to his bowl. Progressive weight loss may also be a symptom of renal failure, liver disease, cancer, hyperthyroidism, or other types of illnesses. It is therefore necessary to keep track of your cat's weight, and notify your vet if you notice any significant changes.

Further, to ensure that your cat receives all the nutrients he needs from his food, whatever brand you buy should meet the requirements of the Association of American Feed Control Officials (AAFCO). The label should state this clearly. Depending on your cat's needs, his veterinarian may also recommend vitamin and mineral supplements.

Exercise

With age, cats tend to become less mobile. Arthritis sometimes sets in, unexercised muscles may begin to lose their strength and elasticity, and circulation generally deteriorates. Regular exercise is therefore just as necessary for an older cat as for a middle-aged cat. Naturally, he will not be able to run about as vigorously as in his prime, but a quiet bit of string chasing or ball batting will serve nicely. Massage can also stimulate blood flow, while relieving soreness and improving muscle tone. It can be very relaxing to pamper your cat this way — particularly if you light a candle and put a little Chopin on the stereo.

Grooming

Because the digestive tract of an older cat tends to lose its elasticity, it is especially important to prevent the accumulation of hair balls. Otherwise, his intestines can become obstructed, and waste matter can accumulate, causing toxic reactions. Daily grooming also affords you an opportunity to examine your cat for lumps and lesions. Anything unusual should be promptly reported to the vet before the condition has a chance to develop any further.

Teeth and claws need special attention as well. Older cats tend to resent the work involved in using a scratching post, and bending over to gnaw the back claws can be downright painful. A weekly trimming session can keep the claws in shape. Daily plaque removal, meanwhile, can help prevent tooth and gum disease. Once a year, the vet should perform a complete exam and cleaning. During the office exam, ask your vet how to go about cleaning your cat's teeth at home between visits.

Sensitivity

Older cats often become increasingly attached to their home environment. They like things just so, and may become extremely upset if too many changes are made. This doesn't mean you can't redecorate if you're tired of the clean, postmodern look. Bringing a new pet into the home or changing residence may, however, cause severe emotional distress. In such cases, he will need a great deal more affection and attention to redress the balance. Similarly, boarding an older cat for even a short period may cause him to become vicious, spiteful, or even disoriented. It's far kinder to everyone to make arrangements for someone to stay with him in his own home, or at least check in with him two or three times a day.

Because they can't tolerate the normal activities of daily life as they once used to, older cats may withdraw or hide. It can be difficult to watch the creature who has shared your life for so long slowly begin to detach. In truth, he does not wish to be ignored, but craves attention of a more soothing nature. If he is open to contact, make it a point of stroking him more frequently, and talking gently to him whenever you pass.

You can also make life easier for him by lifting him onto the bed at night if he sleeps with you. You might also provide "steps" for him to reach his favorite thrones or resting places. Serve his favorite foods, and hand-feed him from time to time, as a way to encourage his appetite and show that you care. After all, the extra burden is not one you'll have to bear for long.

Age-Related Illnesses

While it is possible that your cat may remain vigorous and healthy in old age, chances are that he will suffer from many of the same maladies that affect people as they age. His immune system may begin to weaken, making him more susceptible to disease; coughs and colds are not uncommon; and infections may take longer to heal. More severe problems, meanwhile, can arise from degeneration of the internal organs. Among the more common complaints of aging are:

Cancer. The possibility of developing tumors or lesions increase with age. Females that have never been spayed, or spayed late in life, are especially likely to develop breast cancer. Chemotherapy or surgery may alleviate some of the discomfort associated with the disease, but rarely produce complete remission.

Heart Disease. Symptoms of heart disease include lethargy, loss of appetite, and sleepiness. Since these are also normal signs of old age, they may easily be overlooked until the heart and circulation have degenerated beyond repair. Keep an eye out for more specific symptoms, such as a habit of lying flat on the chest, panting, breathing with an open mouth, occasional paralysis of the back legs, and a bluish cast to the tongue.

Liver Disease. Like any organ, the liver may degenerate with advancing age. Symptoms of liver malfunction include jaundice, vomiting, poor appetite, listlessness, difficulty walking, and dizziness. While liver disease is nearly impossible to cure, medications and dietary management as prescribed by a veterinarian can help reduce the signs of disease.

Renal Failure. The most common signs of kidney disease are weight loss, loss of appetite, bad breath, increased thirst, frequent urination, and occasional vomiting. Symptoms are caused by an accumulation of toxic wastes. Medication and a reduced protein diet can sometimes minimize the effects of toxic accretion. Specially formulated foods can usually be prescribed by a veterinarian.

Diabetes. Excessive thirst, voracious appetite, and heavy urination may point to an insulin imbalance. The problem can be controlled by a change of diet and daily medication. It's a good idea to keep a bottle of corn syrup handy, in case your cat's blood sugar drops severely.

Hyperthyroidism. Sudden weight loss, increased appetite and thirst, hyperactivity, and prodigious bowel movements and urination may signal an overactive thyroid gland. The dysfunction can usually be successfully treated with drugs, radiation, surgery, or a combination of the three.

Digestive Disorders. Irregularity is perhaps one of the most common complaints of old age. In most cases, the treatment is the same for a cat as for a person: bulk. Mixing wheat bran or other sources of fiber may alleviate the problem and also reduce hair balls. Surgery may be required for some obstructions.

DEATH

Sometimes, a cat may die quite suddenly, without displaying any symptoms of distress or illness; other times, symptoms manifest only after a disease has entered its final stages. Such abrupt ends may exact a greater emotional toll on an owner than a more gradual decline. It's difficult to prepare for the loss of a cat, no matter how aloof or irascible she was in life. Often, those who seem to grieve the most are those who thought of their cats as "just pets." They can't measure the love they've had until they've lost it.

When a cat appears unresponsive to touch, when she suddenly becomes limp, when she seems to stare, not at you, but through you — you may justifiably suspect that death is near. If she is in pain, unable to breathe normally, or unlikely to resume normal functioning, the kindest course is to allow your veterinarian to assist her to a quiet, painless end. It is not an easy decision to make, but one must temper hope of miraculous recovery with concern that your cat no longer suffer in this world.

The vet may first administer a sedative, such as Valium, to calm your cat if she's agitated. Afterwards, a large dose of pain-killing medication will swiftly, painlessly carry her to her final rest. During this process, it will be important for you and your cat if you stroke her and talk to her. Hearing is the last sense to fade, and it will be a comfort in the days to come if you know that her last experience on this earth is your voice, letting her know how much you love her, and how much her company has meant.

APPENDICES

Appendix A: Registries and Publications
Registries:
The American Cat Fanciers Association
P.O. Box 203
Point Lookout, MO 65726
Tel: (417) 334-5430
Fax: (417) 334-5540
http://www.acfacat.com/

The Cat Fanciers' Association, Inc.
P.O. Box 1005
Manasquan, NJ 08736-0805
Tel: (908) 528-9797
Fax: (908) 528-7391
http://www.cfainc.org/cfa/

The International Cat Association
P.O. Box 2684
Harlingen, TX 78551
Tel: (210) 428-8046
http://www.tica.org/tica.htm

Publications:
CATS Magazine
29 N. Wacker Dr.
Chicago, IL 60606
Tel: (800) 829-9125

Cat Fancy
Subscription Dept.
P.O. Box 52864
Boulder, CO 80323-2864

Cat Fanciers' Almanac
P.O. Box 1005
Manasquan, NJ 08736-0805

The International Cat Association TREND
P.O. Box 2684
Harlingen, TX 78551

Appendix B: Pet Insurance

Your veterinarian or your local animal shelter or hospital may be able to discuss insurance plans that help to defray the costs of emergency and major medical care. Benefits vary according to each plan, and may be limited to member veterinarians or clinics. Basic plans typically cost about $100 per year, in exchange for percentage reductions in costs. Limits may apply, and you will probably have to pay for certain exclusions and deductibles.

If your veterinarian or clinic cannot advise you, you may choose to contact one of the following organizations for more information:

RLI Planned Services Inc.
Dept. CF
9025 N. Lindbergh Drive
Peoria, IL 61615

Pet Assure Inc.
Sales Department
15 Penn Plaza. OF-2
New York, NY 10001
Tel: (888) 789-PETS

Anipals, Inc.
899 S. College Mall Rd. #242
Bloomington, IN 47401
Tel: (888) ANIPALS

Appendix C: Toxic Substances

Food. Chocolate; caffeine; pork; raw meat; anything rotten, moldy, or suspiciously aged.

Medications. Acetaminophen (Tylenol); antihistamines; aspirin (except as directed by a veterinarian); benzocaine (topical anesthetic); benzyl alcohol; diet pills; heart preparations; hexachlorophene (found in medicated soaps, such as pHiso-Hex); ibuprofen; methylene blue; methyl salicylate; phenazopyridine; phenytoin (Dilantin); phosphate enemas; sleeping pills; tranquilizers; vitamins; anything smelling of wintergreen.

Chemical substances:

Rat/roach poisons:
Strychnine; sodium fluoroacetate; zinc phosphide; warfarin (also prescribed in anticoagulants for people); phosphorous (also found in fireworks, matches, matchboxes, and fertilizers).

Slug/snail bait, ant traps, weed killers, and insecticides: Arsenic; metaldehyde.

Household cleaning agents: Carbamates, chlorinated hydrocarbons; corrosives (e.g., household cleaners, drain openers, solvents); phenol; phosphates; pine oil.

Other common household chemicals: Antifreeze; lead (found in commercial paints, linoleum, and batteries); petroleum products (e.g., gasoline, kerosene, turpentine).

Plants:
Topical allergic reactions: Chrysanthemum; creeping fig, weeping fig; pot mum; spider mum.

Fatal swelling of the mouth, tongue and/or throat: Arrowhead vine; boston ivy; caladium; dumbcane; emerald duke; marble queen; nephthytis; parlor ivy; pathos; philodendron; red princess.

Vomiting, abdominal pain, cramps, and heart, respiratory and/or kidney problems: Amaryllis; azalea; bird of paradise; bittersweet; castor bean; crown of thorns; daffodil; delphinium; elephant ears; foxglove; ground cherry; Indian turnip; ivy; larkspur; poke weed; pot mum; skunk cabbage; soap berry; spider mum; umbrella plant; wisteria.

Various toxic effects, including vomiting, diarrhea, and convulsions: Angel's trumpet; buttercup; chinaberry; coriaria; Dutchman's-breeches; halogeton; jasmine; lily of the valley; locoweed; lupine; marijuana; matrimony vine; mayapple; moonseed; moonweed; morning glory; mushrooms; nightshade; nutmeg; nux vomica; periwinkle; peyote; pig weed; poison hemlock; rhubarb; spinach; sunburned potatoes; water hemlock.

Toxic shrubbery and trees: Almond; American yew; apricot; balsam pear; black locust; cherry; English holly; English yew; horse chestnut/buckeye; Japanese plum; mock orange; peach; privet; rain tree/monkey pod; western yew; wild cherry.

Greenhouse plants: Many plants purchased from a commercial greenhouse have been sprayed with chemical pesticides. Always ask what sprays have been used, how long the spray lasts, and whether or not the leaves and stems can be cleaned; you may also request material safety data for all chemicals used.

Nonpoisonous Plants. African violets; aloe vera; asparagus fern (any of the true ferns are safe); begonias; catnip; coleus; cyclamens; geranium; impatiens; miniature roses; mint; prayer plant; shrimp plant; spider plant; tulips; wandering jew.